How to use E

1 Find a time you can read the Bible each day

2 Find a place where you can be quiet and think

3 Ask God to help you understand

4 Carefully read through the Bible passage for today

5 Study the verses with Explore, taking time to think

6 Pray about what you have read

In this issue

The 92 daily readings in this issue of *Explore* are designed to help you understand and apply the Bible as you read it each day.

It's serious!

We suggest that you allow 15 minutes each day to work through the Bible passage with the notes. It should be a meal, not a snack! Readings from other parts of the Bible can throw valuable light on the study passage. These cross-references can be skipped if you are already feeling full up, but will expand your grasp of the Bible. *Explore* uses the NIV2011 Bible translation, but you can also use it with the NIV1984 or ESV translations.

Sometimes a prayer box will encourage you to stop and pray through the lessons—but it is always important to allow time to pray for God's Spirit to bring his word to life, and to shape the way we think and live through it.

We're serious!

All of us who work on *Explore* share a passion for getting the Bible into people's lives. We fiercely hold to the Bible as God's word— to honour and follow, not to explain away.

thegoodbook COMPANY

Opening up the Bible

Welcome

Tim Thornborough is the Publishing Director at The Good Book Company

Being a Christian isn't a skill you learn, like cooking or stone skipping. Nor is it a lifestyle choice, like the kind of clothes you wear, or the people you choose to hang out with. It's about having a real relationship with the living God through his Son, Jesus Christ. The Bible tells us that this relationship is like a marriage.

It's important to start with this, because many Christians view the practice of daily Bible-reading as a Christian duty, or a hard discipline that is just one more thing to get done in our busy modern lives.

But the Bible is God speaking to us: opening his mind to us on how he thinks, what he wants for us and what his plans are for the world. And most importantly, it tells us what he has done for us in sending his Son, Jesus Christ, into the world. It's the way the Spirit shows Jesus to us, and changes us as we gaze upon his glory.

The Bible is not a manual. It's a love letter. And as with any love letter, we'll want to treasure it, and make time to read and re-read it, so we know we are loved, and discover how we can please the One who loves us. Here are a few suggestions for making your daily time with God more of a joy than a burden:

◆ *Time:* Find a time when you will not be disturbed, and when the cobwebs are cleared from your mind. Many people have found that the morning is the best time as it sets you up for the day. If you're not a "morning person", then last thing at night or a mid-morning break might suit you better. Whatever works for you is right for you.

◆ *Place:* Jesus says that we are not to make a great show of our religion (*see Matthew 6 v 5-6*), but rather, to pray with the door to our room shut. Some people plan to get to work a few minutes earlier and get their Bible out in an office, break room or some other quiet corner.

◆ *Prayer:* Although *Explore* helps with specific prayer ideas from the passage, you should try to develop your own lists to pray through. Use the flap inside the back cover to help with this. And allow what you read in the Scriptures to shape what you pray for yourself, for the world and for others.

◆ *Share:* As the saying goes: *expression deepens impression*. So try to cultivate the habit of sharing with others what you have learned. Why not join our Facebook group (links below) to share your encouragements, questions and prayer requests? Search for *Explore: For your daily walk with God.*

And remember, *it's quality, not quantity, that counts:* better to think briefly about a single verse than to skim through pages without absorbing anything, because it's about developing your relationship with the living God. The sign that your daily time with God is real is when you start to love him more and serve him more wholeheartedly.

Join the Explore Facebook discussion group: facebook.com/groups/tgbc.explore

TITUS: Truth transforms

What does it look like to live for God in the church and the world? Paul's letter to Titus shows us how the truth about Jesus empowers us to live for him.

Welcome to Crete!

Paul and Titus had recently been to Crete, not on holiday, but to plant and grow churches (see Titus 1:5). The big question when Paul left was how the fledgling churches would stay strong in Jesus and live for him. In this first session, we'll get our bearings on the letter before diving into the details.

Who's writing?

Read Titus 1:1-4

- ❓ *What do you notice about the way Paul describes himself in verse 1?*
- ❓ *What does he say his task is?*
- ❓ *In verse 4, what does Paul say about Titus? What do you think he means by this?*

Titus was a trusted colleague of Paul's. His mission, as we'll see, was to establish the churches on Crete by appointing godly leaders (Titus 1:5).

Who's listening?

Paul was writing to Titus. But Titus was responsible for several different churches in Crete. Titus 3:15 sees Paul greet other believers in Crete. And when Paul says, "Grace be with you all", he means the whole church, not simply Titus as an individual. So the letter is written with the Cretan believers in mind too.

Read Titus 2:1-6; 3:1-2

- ❓ *What do we discover about the believers in the Cretan churches?*
- ❓ *In what ways are the Cretan believers like the believers in your church?*
- ❓ *How does this help us as we come to study Titus and apply its message?*
- ❓ *How does Paul describe Titus's job?*

What's the point?

One of the things we will learn is that the good news of forgiveness in Jesus transforms and empowers us to live for Jesus in the church and the world. Two key passages in Titus, 2:11-14 and 3:3-8, will show us the amazing power of God to change our lives and how wonderful the news about Jesus really is—even for sinful people like first-century Cretans and us!

Read Titus 3:8

- ❓ *This verse is a good summary of the letter. What is the heart of Paul's message in this verse?*

🔺 Prayer

Spend some time thanking God for this letter. Pray that God would enable you to understand his message in Titus and help you to see how it applies to your life.

Truth leads to godliness

Being a Christian is more than simply knowing true things. That knowledge must lead to a change of life. That is the key theme to this letter.

God's grace

Read Titus 1:1-4

Paul calls himself a servant and an apostle: two titles which show his humility and authority. He's God's messenger with God's message.

> ❷ *What is Paul's God-given role?*

☑ Apply

The phrase "God's elect" means "God's chosen people". It speaks of his grace and mercy in taking the initiative to save us to be his people. God's election of his people can be a baffling and profound truth to think about. But why is this an encouraging truth for Paul to start the letter with? If God didn't take the initiative to save us, how then can we be saved from our sin? (For help, see Titus 3:4-5; Ephesians 1:3-6.)

> ❷ *How might this truth help you when you're feeling weary, hard-pressed or discouraged in your Christian life? Or when your church family is going through a hard time?*

In verse 1 Paul speaks of "the truth that leads to godliness". "Godliness" simply means living God's way.

> ❷ *Why is it important that truth and godliness stay together?*
> ❷ *What happens if you only have one or the other?*

God's promise

Re-read Titus 1:1-4

> ❷ *How does Paul describe the believer's hope in verse 2?*
> ❷ *How do we know this will happen?*
> ❷ *How can we know this hope according to verse 3?*

Paul describes in these few verses a remarkable picture of what God does in eternity past and eternity future. It's an amazing picture of the beauty and joy of the Christian life. Believers are chosen in eternity past for an eternal future with him.

☑ Apply

> ❷ *How does this picture of true Christianity help us when faced by the brokenness of the world we live in, and by the hostility of the non-Christian world?*
> ❷ *If God uses human preaching and speaking about Jesus to bring people to faith in him, how should this impact the way we view our evangelism?*

◤ Pray

Praise God for his grace and mercy to us in Jesus, from eternity past to eternity future. Pray for courage to share this great gospel.

Raise the praise!

Time for a psalm sandwich. The pieces of bread at the beginning and end are short sections praising God (v 1-3) and trusting God (v 20-22).

This sandwich has two fillings: sections on God the Ruler (v 4-11) and God the Judge (v 12-19). Let's take a big bite...

Praising God
Read Psalm 33:1-3

> ❷ *How would you describe the character of the praise we should offer to God?*
> ❷ *Is that what your praise looks and feels like?*

Psalms are meant to be lived and experienced, not just studied. So why not respond to the call of these verses to praise God with enthusiastic abandon. You could sing a favourite hymn or song if you like—mine is *Praise to the Lord, the Almighty, the King of creation,* but you can choose your own.

God the Ruler
Read Psalm 33:4-11

This is the awesome, astounding God we serve. His word (by which he rules all things) is right and true (v 4). Perfect, in fact. He is dependably faithful. His unfailing love fills the earth (v 5; Psalm 36:5-9), which he so perfectly created (Psalm 33:6-9), and over which he is sovereign (v 10-11). This is the God of the whole world, and so everyone, everywhere owe their existence and praise to him.

> ❷ *How do you think God feels that so many neither fear nor revere him?*

God the Judge
Read Psalm 33:12-19

God chose one people (Israel) to be his inheritance (v 12). Since Jesus died and rose again, all who trust in him are included in this inheritance.

God sees all of humankind. He sees beyond our appearance, right into our hearts (v 13-15). We are under review, and nothing anyone has (position, power, strength) can save them from death (v 16-17).

> ❷ *So who can know God (v 18)? Who are his people?*
> ❷ *What will God do for them (v 19)?*

Trusting God
Read Psalm 33:20-22

As God's people we have a confident hope (expectation), not only of eternity with him but a hope that assures us that he is our help and our shield (v 20). So we can fully trust God because of what he has revealed about himself: his holy name (v 21). And we can rejoice in him (v 21) and praise him for all that he is. Which brings us back to where we came in—praising God.

Read slowly through Psalm 33 once more, joyfully praising the Lord for everything he is to us and everything he faithfully does for us, remembering our reverent response to him (v 8).

Unfinished business

The first thing on Paul's agenda is leadership in the church. Godly leaders are vital for a godly church.

Godly lives

Read Titus 1:5-9

- ❓ *What does Paul say about a leader's home life in verse 6?*
- ❓ *Why is a leader's private life a matter of concern?*
- ❓ *What other qualities should a leader have according to verses 7-8?*
- ❓ *How might someone with the qualities of verse 7 be a danger to a church?*
- ❓ *How might someone with the qualities of verse 8 be a blessing?*

Paul has already told us that the truth leads to godliness, and that the life-changing truth about Jesus is entrusted to us to pass on. Paul therefore is very concerned that churches have godly and faithful leaders to lead them. He calls them elders in verse 5, which simply means those given leadership responsibility in a church. Christians won't grow into godliness unless they have good leaders teaching the truth and living godly lives. Godly leadership is vital for our spiritual growth. Paul's criteria for leadership though are different from the world's. There's no mention here of leadership skills and management style. Paul is more concerned about a godly life and faithful teaching. Leaders must teach and model the faith. These are the leaders we need.

- ❓ *Recent failures of prominent Christian leaders have shone a spotlight on this issue: what can we learn here on this?*

Faithful teaching

- ❓ *What is the leader's main task, according to Paul in verse 9?*
- ❓ *What will this task involve in practice?*
- ❓ *Why must a leader hold firmly to the trustworthy message?*

☑ Apply

Leaders are a working example how truth leads to godliness. They teach and live the truth for the good of the church, and so must the members of the church. The qualities of leaders are also required of all Christians as they follow Jesus. We'll see in Titus 2:1-10 that many of the same qualities are applied to all the congregation.

- ❓ *Looking at these qualities of leadership and the Christian life in general, what areas do you think you need to work on with God's help?*
- ❓ *How might Paul's words here help those who appoint leaders at church?*
- ❓ *How do these verses help you to pray for your leaders?*

⌃ Pray

Pray for your church leaders by name and ask the Lord to help them grow in godly and faithful teaching.

Watch out!

All is not well in Crete. Danger lurks in the churches. So Titus must take firm action.

Ungodly teachers!

Read Titus 1:10-16

❓ *What does Paul say about these false teachers in verse 10?*

❓ *What effect are they having on the churches, verse 11?*

❓ *What is their character like according to verse 12?*

It's easy to think that the job of a good leader is simply to teach the truth and show people how to live godly lives. But that's not the whole task. Good leaders must also refute wrong teaching and wrong living. Notice the "for" at the start of verse 10.

The churches in Crete need godly leaders because there are ungodly leaders in the churches. Paul says that these teachers are "of the circumcision group". These are probably Jewish leaders who claim to be Christians, but who are wanting the non-Jewish believers in Crete to follow Jewish laws too, like circumcision and eating the right foods. Paul is very clear in Titus that all you need to become and then to live as a Christian is to trust in what Jesus has already done for you on the cross! See Titus 2:14 and 3:4-5. You don't need to follow extra rules and laws.

Paul isn't being racist in Titus 1:12. He simply quotes a Cretan poet who is making a general statement about Cretan character and culture. He's saying, "These people are just like the stereotype".

Ungodly lifestyles

In verse 13 Paul seems to be addressing the Christians affected by the false teachers.

❓ *What does he tell Titus to do?*

❓ *What will be the outcome if he does?*

❓ *Verses 15-16 revert back to the ungodly teachers. How is verse 16 a useful summary of this whole passage?*

⌄ Apply

❓ *Why is Paul so serious about the dangers of false teaching?*

❓ *What is the link between false teaching and false living?*

❓ *How does this help us to see more clearly the link between true teaching and true living?*

Paul talks about rebuking Christians who are going astray in verse 13.

❓ *Do you think such actions have a place in our churches today?*

❓ *What makes church discipline so difficult to administrate today?*

❓ *How can the rebuking or correcting of other Christians be done in such a way as to build them up, not tear them down?*

❓ *Why is this an important part of our pastoral care for one another?*

Family matters

What does godly living look like in practice? Paul tells Titus to teach his church family to live according to their age…

Godly living for all ages
Read Titus 2:1-5

At the end of chapter 1 Paul exposed the dangers of false teaching and living. Now he says Titus must teach "sound doctrine" to his congregation. The word for "sound" is literally "healthy". Such godly teaching builds the churches' spiritual health. What we see in this passage is teaching appropriate to the different age groups in the churches in Crete. Different ages face different challenges. But we'll also see there should be mutual care and respect between the different generations in a church family.

- ❷ *What does Paul say that Titus should teach the older men in verse 2?*
- ❷ *Why do you think Paul commands him to teach these specific things?*
- ❷ *What is Titus to teach the older women in verses 3-4?*
- ❷ *Why do you think Paul commands him to teach these specific things?*
- ❷ *In verses 3-5 the younger women are also addressed. But it's the older women who are to teach them. Why do you think that is?*
- ❷ *Why do you think Paul commands them to teach these specific things?*

Paul's teaching about younger women isn't meant to exclude women whose marital circumstances are different; nor is he ruling out a working career for women. These are general principles for godly living which need to be applied to each individual person.

⌄ Apply

Paul talks about older women training and modelling godly lives to younger women—and Paul will encourage Titus to do the same for the younger men in verse 7.

- ❷ *Why is this an effective way of teaching the gospel to younger women?*
- ❷ *In some Western cultures, respect for the older generation is waning. How does Paul affirm the role of older members of our churches?*
- ❷ *How could you encourage such godly relationships in your church family?*

In verse 5 Paul says that such godly lives among the women will mean the word of God is not maligned. He assumes that ungodly living will bring the gospel into disrepute.

- ❷ *How might such godly living among older and younger believers promote the gospel in your community?*

⌃ Pray

Pray for yourself, according to your age, that you would live a godly life which promotes the gospel. Think of an older / younger person you could encourage or seek wisdom from and pray for them now.

Godly living in all of life

Living a godly life affects everything we do, even when we're at work!

To the younger men

Read Titus 2:6-8

The churches in Crete were full of many different sorts of people, who were encouraged to support and encourage one another in godly living.

- ❓ *What's the single command that Titus is to give the young men in verse 6?*
- ❓ *Why do you think he says this one thing?*
- ❓ *What is Titus to do himself (v 7-8)?*
- ❓ *How does this teach again the link between truth and godliness?*
- ❓ *How does it reinforce what Paul taught in 1:6-9?*

⌄ Apply

- ❓ *Why is godly role-modelling so important in the Christian life?*
- ❓ *What steps can we take to develop this spiritual mentoring in our church life?*

To the workers

Read Titus 2:9-10

Slaves in the ancient world were numerous—by some estimates up to a third of the population in a typical Roman town. But slavery in the ancient world was very different from the 18th and 19th centuries. It could still be tough, but they were treated more like "owned employees". And so there are parallels to our working environments.

- ❓ *What is Titus to teach slaves?*
- ❓ *What's Paul's reason for this teaching?*

⋯ TIME OUT ⋯

For more help on slaves and masters, look up Paul's teaching in Ephesians 6:5-9.

- ❓ *If you sought to live like this in your workplace, what changes, if any, might you see?*

⌄ Apply

- ❓ *Why do you think Paul spends a good deal of time in Titus urging us to develop godly Christian characteristics?*
- ❓ *Why is this so vital in the church and the world? For help compare the ends of verses 5, 8 and 10 in Titus 2.*
- ❓ *How does this focus on character differ from the world's values?*
- ❓ *How could you encourage more thinking about Christian character in your small group or church family?*

⌃ Pray

Pray that God by his Spirit would help you to develop a godly Christian character.

Pray for your work environment—that you would commend the gospel by the way you work and act.

The engine of holiness

What power is there to live the Christian life? Is it all about trying our best, doing good for the sake of being good?

Paul has explained what godly living looks like for different groups in the church. Now he's going to show us where the power for godly living comes from. *And the answer is...*

Read Titus 2:11-15

❓ *So where does this power come from?*

Paul speaks about two "appearings" of Jesus. In verse 11, he says that "the grace of God has appeared". This is referring to the first coming of Jesus, when he lived, died and rose again. "Appearing of the glory" (v 13), is the second coming of Jesus at the end of time. We live in between those two appearings. And we live in the light of them both.

First appearing: all about grace

❓ *What does Paul say about the appearing of grace in verse 11?*

❓ *What does it teach us (v 12)?*

Paul explains a bit more about this first appearing in verse 14. In what ways does this verse help us understand more clearly how the first appearing teaches us to "say 'no' to ungodliness"?

⌄ Apply

❓ *How would you help a friend who said they thought the Christian life was all about rules and self-improvement?*

❓ *How does Paul's teaching in verses 11-12 and 14 help you in the struggle for holiness?*

Second appearing: all about glory

❓ *What does Paul say we're waiting for in verse 13?*

❓ *How is Jesus' second coming going to be different from his first?*

❓ *How does this second appearing motivate you for godly living?*

❓ *How can you make sure this second appearing is part of your thinking on a regular basis?*

⌄ Apply

❓ *Why is it vital that the first and second appearings of Jesus are taught regularly in our churches?*

❓ *What motivation for godly living would we have if these things weren't taught?*

❓ *How has this passage helped and encouraged you in the battle for holiness in your personal life?*

⌃ Pray

Thank God for the first coming of Jesus to save us.

Pray you'd live a godly life empowered by grace, looking forward to the future coming of Jesus.

Transforming society?

The Christian life is not simply about personal holiness. The way we live can impact others for good.

All the way through the letter to Titus, Paul has been reminding the churches in Crete to promote the gospel by the way they live. The truth of the gospel should lead to godly living.

In Titus 2:5, older women were to teach younger women to be subject to their husbands, "so that no one will malign the word of God". In verse 8, younger men were to be godly in speech, so their opponents won't have anything bad to say about them. And in verse 10 slaves were to be godly at work because such godly counter-cultural living makes the teaching about Jesus attractive. Godly believers promote the gospel to the world around them. The challenge is to live such lives!

Submitting

Read Titus 3:1-2

- ❷ *What does Paul tell Titus to remind the people to do in verse 1?*
- ❷ *What do you think he means by his phrase "do whatever is good"?*

···· TIME OUT ····

Look up Romans 13:1-5. Paul says a bit more about submitting to authorities in these verses.

- ❷ *What reasons does Paul give for submitting to governing authorities?*
- ❷ *What will such godly submission mean for you in your own country?*

- ❷ *How will this promote the gospel?*
- ❷ *Do you think there are times when godly submission is not the right thing to do? If so, when might these be and how would such actions also promote the gospel?*

Good neighbours!

- ❷ *Why do you think Paul adds his instructions in Titus 3:2?*
- ❷ *In what situations could we find ourselves where we're tempted to slander others or be harsh with others?*

It's important to remember that Paul is not simply addressing us as individuals. He's speaking to the whole church family in Crete. He addresses us as gathered communities saved by the grace of Jesus.

- ❷ *How might such a godly witness as a whole church community promote the gospel in the area around your church?*

⌃ Pray

Pray that God would give you the strength and courage to live a godly life as you submit to the governing authorities. Pray for your local community to be impacted by the way your church lives.

How to face a crisis

Many of us feel we have faced more than our fair share of problems these last two years. And yet, all over the world, our fellow believers face daily physical threat and constant pressure to renounce Christ. How do we face problems great and small?

David was on the run from Saul and sought refuge with Abimelech (*aka* Achish, see 1 Samuel 21:10-14), the Philistine King. Afraid of being recognised, David pretended to be a madman, and they released him. But David realised it wasn't his own guile that kept him safe...

Hands and lips

Read Psalm 34:1-7

David recognises God's hand in his deliverance, and gives God the praise he is due. In fact, David commits himself to continual praise of the Lord (v 1). He acknowledges that it wasn't his own doing, but that God rescued him when he was at the bottom of life's heap (v 6).

⊻ Apply

❷ *Why is it that we're more likely to call out to God or give him the glory when we're at our lowest?*

❷ *Do you recognise and acknowledge God's unseen hand at work in your daily life?*

❷ *Do you give him the praise he is due?*

Secret of a good life

Read Psalm 34:8-14

Just savour verse 8. Do you want to see God's goodness? Then get to know him.

Next, David gives us the secret of a good life: give God the fear and reverence he

deserves (v 9, 11) and you will find him to be sufficient for everything you want or need (v 9-10).

❷ *How can we show fear of the Lord (v 11-14)?*

❷ *What's the difference between simply wanting peace and seeking peace and pursuing it (v 14)?*

Prayer in crisis

Read Psalm 34:15-22

David shows us how God treats those who fear him (*the righteous*—v 15, 17, 19) and also those who do evil (v 16, 21). In fact, the wicked are so thoroughly dealt with that they become totally forgotten (v 16).

Tough times are to be met with prayer, crying out to the Lord (v 17) who looks after his people in times of trouble (v 17), broken-heartedness (v 18) and pain. The Lord is close to his suffering people. Not just nearby, but actively making our troubles his own, protecting (v 20), delivering (v 19), fighting for (v 21) and redeeming (v 22) his children.

⌃ Pray

Psalm 34 is a brilliant lesson in how to react to crises in our lives. Pray for those you know who are struggling at the moment. Pray specifically that the attitudes and responses of this psalm would be theirs as well.

Amazing love!

To be loved and appreciated is a wonderful thing. To be loved by God himself is nothing short of astonishing and transformative.

Our big problem
Read Titus 3:3-8

- ❓ *What does Paul say is our big problem in verse 3?*
- ❓ *Why is it important to have a right view of this problem?*
- ❓ *How does it help us as we seek to share our faith with friends and family?*

This passage is one of the highlights of the short letter to Titus. It's packed full of remarkable truths about what God has done for us in Christ. Paul begins in verse 3 with a major problem we all have. Notice he says "we". He includes himself in this, and is implying that by nature we're no better than anyone else.

God's big solution

- ❓ *Why has God saved us (v 4-5)?*
- ❓ *Given verse 3, why is it necessary for God to do this?*
- ❓ *How is the Holy Spirit involved in this great task?*

···· TIME OUT ····

Verses 4-7 are densely packed with great truths. If you have time, write out each verse in your own words to help you understand what Paul is saying. Notice how God is taking the initiative in everything. It's nothing to do with us!

- ❓ *What is the result of this gracious and loving action in verse 7?*

The heart of this passage is in verse 5, where Paul says we're saved not by works but by God's mercy. We don't deserve to be rescued and loved. But the amazing truth is that, through Jesus, God pours out his blessings on his people—his love, his Spirit, his forgiveness and his promise of the future.

⌄ Apply

- ❓ *How is the description of God and his actions different from what you sometimes think of him?*

In verse 8, Paul wants Titus to stress these things. He says that "these things", meaning the glorious truths of verses 3-7, are "excellent and profitable for everyone".

- ❓ *What's his reason for stressing these things? Why does this again strengthen the link between the truth about Jesus and godly living?*

⌃ Pray

Write down three great truths from this passage and thank God for them. Thank God too for his character, his love, mercy and grace.

Pray for a couple of friends to come to know the loving and gracious God themselves.

Staying focused

It's easy to be distracted from the good news of Jesus. How can we stay focused on what is good and right?

Paul has been telling Titus about the love and kindness of God. Paul told Titus to stress these things (v 8). Titus's focus was to be on the good news of Jesus and the loving mercy of God. Now, Paul shows Titus how to deal with two issues that might distract him from this gospel focus: avoiding foolish controversies and dealing with divisive people. Both things can be hugely time-consuming and hard to deal with in church life today.

What to avoid

Read Titus 3:9-11

❷ *What does Paul tell Titus to avoid in verse 9?*
❷ *Why should Titus do this?*

It's possible some of these controversies were to do with the false teachers and leaders that we saw in Titus 1:10-11. There we saw that some so-called Christians from a Jewish background were seeking to impose Jewish law on the non-Jewish Cretan believers. It's easy to get sucked into debates about theological controversies which are unhelpful and distracting, especially on the internet.

❷ *What sort of things could distract you from your focus on the good news of Jesus?*
❷ *How can you spot the difference between wise engagement with wrong ideas and unhelpful distraction?*

Who to warn

We've been reminded throughout Titus that being a Christian is not simply an individual experience. Believers are to be part of a church community to help and encourage one another. So those who upset the unity of the church can be a danger.

It seems that Paul is concerned not simply with small disagreements which happen in every church family. Rather his focus is those who deliberately seek to divide people for various reasons—power, pride, even spite perhaps. Action needs to be taken for the sake of gospel unity and witness in the church.

❷ *What is Paul's advice to Titus (v 10)?*
❷ *Why does he say this (v 11)?*

TIME OUT

Look up Matthew 18:15-17. Jesus' teaching helps us understand a bit more about how to deal with these issues in church life.

❷ *Why is such godly and gracious discipline good and important for church life?*

⌃ Pray

Pray for grace to stay focused on the gospel, and that our churches might be places of gospel unity and love.

Partnering together

The Christian life is not about being a solo operator. It's about partnering with others for our good and for the glory of Jesus.

If you've read other letters of Paul, you'll know that he often includes names of friends and colleagues at the end of his letters. It's easy to skip over these as if they were irrelevant or boring. In fact, they reveal a great deal about Paul and the way he served God and people. He's a man who partners with others and needs others' support and encouragement in the work of the gospel. These final verses in Titus are no different.

Gospel partnership
Read Titus 3:12-15

- ❷ *What does Paul ask Titus to do?*
- ❷ *What does this show about Paul's attitude to his friends and colleagues?*
- ❷ *Paul's greetings in verse 15 are also instructive. What do they show us about Paul's relationships?*

···· TIME OUT ····························

We don't know anything more about Artemas or Zenas. But Tychicus and Apollos were key colleagues for Paul. Tychicus helped in the churches in Ephesus and Colossae; Apollos helped Paul in Corinth. **Look up Colossians 4:7-8 and 1 Corinthians 3:5-9** to find out more about them.

▼ Apply

Often we can be jealous of the success of others' ministries or gifts. Or we can unhelpfully compare ourselves to others and look down on others.

- ❷ *How do Paul's words in Titus 3 challenge such jealousies?*
- ❷ *Think about the key truths you've learned from your studies in Titus. How can these truths stop you falling into these jealousies and instead serve God's people with love?*

Gospel living
Re-read Titus 3:14-15

Paul's final words to Titus sum up his key message for the Cretan churches.

- ❷ *What is Paul's concern for the Cretan believers?*
- ❷ *What do you think Paul means by "good" here? (For help, remember 1:8; 2:14; 3:8.)*
- ❷ *Given all we've seen in Titus, how can a believer live a productive life? What might an unproductive life look like?*

▲ Pray

Thank God for other believers you serve with. Pray for yourself to serve with godly love and with no hint of jealousy or pride.

Titus revisited

A message is only truly understood if it leads to action. That's certainly true of the letter to Titus.

In our final study in the book of Titus we're going to take some time to revisit some key lessons so that Paul's message gets right into our hearts.

❓ *How would you sum up the message of Titus in a short sentence?*

The heart of the matter

Read Titus 1:1-4

Paul began his letter by telling Titus that the truth about Jesus must lead to a changed life. The truth leads to godliness. That's the sign that the truth is fully understand and accepted.

❓ *Why is Paul so keen to connect the truth of the gospel with a godly life?*
❓ *Looking through the letter again, how was this principle to be seen in the leaders Titus appointed on Crete? For help see verses 6-9.*
❓ *How was the same principle to be seen in the lives of Titus's congregation? For example, among young men and slaves? For help see 2:6-10.*

⌄ Apply

Think about this principle of the truth leading to godliness:

❓ *In what areas of your life have you felt challenged as you've read this letter?*
❓ *How can you make sure you don't forget or ignore those challenges?*

The good news

Read Titus 2:11-14 and 3:3-7

The gospel is the central truth that drives everything else in the Christian life. We can't change by ourselves. We need God to change us and to empower us to live for him.

❓ *Using these passages to help you, why is the good news about Jesus such good news?*
❓ *What have you learned about God's character through these passages?*
❓ *How is the good news of Jesus the engine for you to grow more like him?*
❓ *Why must we never lose sight of or forget the good news about Jesus?*

Not just "me" but "we"

We've also seen that Titus is addressed not just to an individual but to a group of believers in Crete.

❓ *How has reading Titus challenged your attitude to church and other believers? For example, look up 3:9, 14-15.*

⌃ Pray

Write down three things you've found encouraging from Titus and three things you've found challenging. Thank God for the encouragements and pray about the challenges.

1 KINGS: Who will be king?

David is an old man and doesn't have long to live. Who will be king after him? Has God chosen the next king?

Meet the king(s)
Read 1 Kings 1:1-10

1 Kings starts where 2 Samuel ends, and many of the people we meet in the first two chapters are familiar from that book: David the king, Bathsheba one of his wives, Nathan the prophet, even Joab the army commander. However, we meet some new characters too, Abishag and Adonijah.

❓ *How does Abishag's role emphasise David's age (v 1-5)?*

❓ *What are Adonijah's qualifications for kingship, if any (v 6-10)?*

❓ *Do you think Adonijah is presented as a good choice as king? Think about why.*

Notice that the narrator does not tell us what he thinks of Adonijah directly. We will need to get used to this as we read 1 Kings. We are often told what happened and left to evaluate it for ourselves based on what we know from God's word.

The Promise
Read 1 Kings 1:11-27

Bathsheba (Solomon's mother) features prominently, as does Nathan the prophet.

❓ *Given their roles in 2 Samuel 11 – 12, what does this remind us about David?*

We are told twice that Nathan wasn't invited to Adonijah's party (1 Kings 1:8, 10), neither was Solomon. Now Nathan puts a plan in place with Bathsheba to make sure that Solomon becomes king.

❓ *What crucial piece of information do we learn in verses 11-14?*

❓ *What does Bathsheba ask David to do (v 15-21)?*

❓ *Why do you think Nathan comes in next and says the same things as Bathsheba (v 22-27)?*

We finish today on a bit of a cliff-hanger—what will happen next? Will David do something? We'll find out tomorrow.

⌄ Apply

This kind of high-courtly politics no doubt feels very removed from most of our lives. But here we meet, as we will throughout 1 Kings, real people like Bathsheba and David with real weaknesses. We see God's plan for Solomon to be king starting to work itself out, even if it all looks a bit precarious at this stage. We are reminded that God works through history, even when it is hard to see what is going on.

❓ *Whose "weakness" do you most identify with today?*

⌃ Pray

Give thanks to God that he can still use us, despite our weaknesses, and that he has a plan.

Solomon the king

Now David acts, and Solomon becomes king, and we hear the new king speak for the first time, as a promise is kept.

David the king

Read 1 Kings 1:28-40

Yesterday finished with a question—will David act? Yes. King David acts decisively.

> ❓ *Why is David's promise to Bathsheba in verses 28-31 important?*
> ❓ *How is David going to make sure that Solomon becomes king (v 32-35)?*
> ❓ *We meet Benaiah for the first time in verses 36-37. What do you think of him?*

David commands, and Nathan, Zadok and Benaiah act (v 38-40). This is one of the ways the narrator in 1 Kings will show us that people are doing the right thing: when they do what God, or here what the king, tells them. The Kerethites and Pelethites are David's personal bodyguard, very loyal to him.

▽ Apply

> ❓ *How do Benaiah's words in verses 36-37 help us to understand what is really going on here?*

Solomon the king

Read 1 Kings 1:41-53

Joab, the old soldier, is the first to hear the trumpet sound. A messenger arrives with news, but it is not good news for Adonijah.

> ❓ *What key things does Jonathan say that show that Adonijah's hopes of being king are dashed (v 43-48)?*

The guests know the game is up (v 49), and hope that a quick exit will save them. We'll see more on this in 1 Kings 2. But what about Adonijah? He goes to the altar and takes hold of it. It is a bit like when people seek sanctuary in a church building. He knows Solomon will be reluctant to come and get him. So, what will Solomon do?

> ❓ *What do you make of Solomon's first words in 1:52-53?*

We meet Solomon for the first time, and we're going to spend a lot of time over the next few days getting to know him. We will keep coming back to this question—what do we make of Solomon? What kind of king is he? So, keep that question in mind day by day.

▽ Apply

Solomon is king. Promises have been kept. Obstacles have been overcome, and we have heard Benaiah's request (v 36-37) that God would be with Solomon as he has been with David.

> ❓ *How does this chapter reassure you that God will keep his promises?*

An air of expectancy

Psalm 35 finds David in another spot of bother. This time he's being maliciously slandered by people he's shown only kindness to.

A mighty warrior
Read Psalm 35:1-3

> ❷ *In what situations could you imagine yourself praying a prayer like this?*
> ❷ *Why might he be asking the Lord to give him the reassuring words of verse 3?*

Unlike the previous few psalms, David doesn't appeal to God as his shield and refuge. He appeals to the Lord as a mighty warrior to fight on his side.

Angry prayer
Read Psalm 35:4-10

> ❷ *Are you shocked at David's words in verses 4-8?*

They're full of anger and a real desire to see his enemies crushed. It may sound like selfish revenge, but David is praying for God's will to be done in punishing their opposition to the Lord's anointed. David is the Lord's anointed king, so any attack on him is also an attack on the Lord and his good purposes. He is not seeking revenge; he is seeking victory, not for his own gratification, but for the Lord's honour.

For us, of course, the Lord's anointed King is Jesus.

> ❷ *Are you angered by opposition to him?*
> ❷ *When you pray, are you seeking victory for him, or are you praying solely towards your own benefit?*

In verses 9-10 David expects his prayer to be answered and promises to give God the due praise and glory.

> ❷ *Do you pray expecting God to answer?*

Honest prayer
Read Psalm 35:11-18

David tells God exactly what's on his mind, what he's going through, and how he feels about God's apparent silence (v 13). Yet he isn't blaming God, and he continues to rely on God to sort out the desperate situation.

For a second time, David promises to praise the Lord when he answers David's cry (v 18).

Expectant prayer
Read Psalm 35:19-28

Again, David asks God to act against his enemies (v 23-26). And again, he shows anticipation that God will act, and he reaffirms his promise to give God the glory (v 28).

> ❷ *Ask God to give you David's attitude: expecting God to answer your prayers.*
> ❷ *Dare you promise to praise God when he does answer your prayers?*

Such promises are not to be taken lightly.

The king is established

Solomon is on the throne, but he is far from secure. There are some things he still needs to deal with, for himself and for David.

Final instructions

Read 1 Kings 2:1-12

We come to David's final instructions to Solomon before his death.

> ❷ *What do David's instructions in verses 1-4 tell us about what is important for a king?*

David's instructions that follow relate to events in 2 Samuel. Joab murdered Abner (2 Samuel 3:26-30) and Amasa (2 Samuel 20:4-13) because they were rivals for his role as commander of David's armies.

> ❷ *What does David's "obituary" (1 Kings 2:10-12) tell us about what kind of king he was?*

Unfinished business

Read 1 Kings 2:13-46

Solomon deals with four people here: Adonijah (v 13-25), Abiathar (v 26-7), Joab (v 28-35) and Shimei (v 36-46). Let's look at each one in turn.

Adonijah comes to Bathsheba and asks for Abishag, David's "bed warmer". This is a problem because one of the ways for a new king to establish himself was to take over the harem or the concubines of the previous king.

> ❷ *What does Solomon's reaction to the request of Adonijah reveal about how secure he feels (v 22-24)?*

Abiathar is sent back to his estate, for his role in the conspiracy to put Adonijah on the throne. He escapes death because of previous loyalty.

> ❷ *How does verse 27 reassure us about what is going on here?*

Joab acts before Solomon can, and like Adonijah in chapter 1 seeks sanctuary beside the altar. But there is no sanctuary from the king's justice through Benaiah.

> ❷ *How does Solomon defend his actions in 1 Kings 2:31-33?*

Finally, **Shimei**. Solomon wants to keep him close at hand in Jerusalem (v 36-38), but Shimei goes after some servants, thus breaking the rules (v 39-41).

> ❷ *Solomon gives two reasons for executing Shimei (v 42-5). Why, do you think?*
> ❷ *We meet Benaiah again in verses 25, 34-5 and 46. What do we make of him?*

Solomon's kingdom is established (v 46). The narrator paints a picture of Solomon in this chapter but leaves us to think about what that picture is. And yet, God's purposes are clearly fulfilled.

⌃ Pray

Give thanks that God keeps his promises and fulfils his plans, even if the human agents aren't always perfect, like Solomon, and like us.

Wisdom given and used

God meets with Solomon and grants him great gifts, which he then uses.

Wisdom granted

Read 1 Kings 3:1-15

The first few verses of this chapter highlight some of the key themes of Solomon's reign: his marriage to foreign women (v 1), his work in building his palace (v 1), and his work in building the temple (v 1-2).

❓ *What do these first few verses of the chapter (v 1-4) tell us about Solomon?*

God appears to Solomon in a dream in verse 5. This highlights Solomon's importance, because God's appearances like this are rare, and God appears twice to Solomon (see 9:2). He invites Solomon to ask for whatever he wants. Solomon asks for wisdom.

❓ *What does Solomon's request in 3:6-9 reveal about his understanding of why he is king?*
❓ *What does God give to Solomon as well as wisdom (v 10-13)?*
❓ *What does Solomon need to do? (v 14)*

▼ Apply

Solomon's request is a good example to us of having the right priorities. It's a good challenge to us to think about how we would answer the same question: "Ask for whatever you want me to give you".

Wisdom in action

Read 1 Kings 3:16-28

Two prostitutes come to the king with a tragic tale. Both have recently had sons, but one has died, and they are disputing whose child is alive and whose is dead.

❓ *What makes this such a difficult case for Solomon to resolve (v 16-23)?*
❓ *Why does Solomon's drastic-sounding solution work (v 24-27)?*

The narrator records the people's response in verse 28, as they recognise the wisdom of the king. We see the first fulfilment of the promise that God made to Solomon, to give him wisdom. As we go through the rest of Solomon's reign in chapters 4 – 11, we will see how the other promises made to Solomon are fulfilled. We will see how he builds his palace and the temple, as well as the impact of his foreign wives on him.

▲ Pray

As we reflect on Solomon's wisdom, pray that our actions might also be marked by godly wisdom.

And pray for the leaders in your church, and also nationally and internationally, to be guided by godly wisdom.

Running the kingdom

Solomon's wisdom is not just academic; it's thoroughly practical. In this chapter we get an insight into how Solomon's kingdom was run under its wise king.

Officials and provisions

Read 1 Kings 4:1-28

Here we meet Solomon's chief officials (v 2-6), and twelve governors who supplied the household month by month (v 7-19).

❷ *How does this information help us to further understand Solomon's wisdom?*

We have met some of these officials before. Zadok, Benaiah and Nathan have been important in 1 Kings 1 – 2.

❷ *What might this tell us about the way Solomon ruled?*

We come to an important summary of Solomon's reign in 4:20-21. The mention of the people "as numerous as the sand on the seashore" recalls God's promise to Abraham in Genesis 22:17 that he would have numerous descendants. The people are blessed by God (we see this also in verse 25). Solomon rules from the Euphrates to Egypt, which is the land promised to Abraham in Genesis 15:18. God has kept his promise to bless his people in his land.

We then come to more on Solomon's daily provisions in 1 Kings 4:22-28.

❷ *How do these verses show that God has kept his promises to Solomon?*
❷ *How would you describe Israel's situation in these verses?*

Pray

Reflect on the "big picture" of God's plans for his people here. Give thanks to God that he has a plan for his people.

Wisest. Man. Ever.

Read 1 Kings 4:29-34

❷ *How is Solomon's wisdom described in these verses? What kind of wisdom is it?*

Apply

As we find out more about the day-to-day running of Solomon's kingdom, we are presented with a very positive picture of Solomon's great wisdom, and his great wealth and honour, just as God promised.

There are also some things here that might make us think. We have a man in charge of forced labour (v 6), lots of food being eaten (v 22-23), and horses and chariots (v 26). If we read some of the passages earlier in the Bible which warn Israel about what kings will be like, such as 1 Samuel 8:11-18, we find that this is how a king could become a burden for Israel.

❷ *Is Solomon's wealth a problem? Or is it only a potential problem?*
❷ *How does this passage challenge your assumptions about wealth and honour?*

Cedars from Lebanon

We now see some of Solomon's preparation for constructing the temple and learn more about his wisdom.

Read 1 Kings 5:1-18

Our passage begins with Hiram king of Tyre writing to Solomon, because he wants to continue the good diplomatic relations between the kingdoms that existed under David (v 1).

❓ *What strikes you about the explanation Solomon gives for why David couldn't build the temple (v 3-5)?*

Solomon needs good strong trees, for the temple—cedars from Lebanon. He also needs help from Hiram's people—Sidonians—to cut them (v 6). Hiram needs food for the royal household (v 8-9), and so the deal is struck, and a treaty is made (v 10-12).

Notice that both Hiram in verse 7 and the narrator in verse 12 draw attention to Solomon's wisdom here.

❓ *What does it mean for Solomon to be wise in this passage?*

···· TIME OUT ··································

In verse 5 we see one of many references in 1 Kings 1 – 11 back to 2 Samuel 7, particularly the promises God made to David in verses 12-16. Take the time to read that passage and reflect on it as we look at 1 Kings 5.

··

We then move to a description of Solomon's conscripted labourers (1 Kings 5:13-14). This involves 30,000 Israelites, in shifts of 10,000 a month. This is not slavery, but it

does impose a significant responsibility on those involved and their families and communities. This kind of practice was common in the ancient world, and so wouldn't be viewed then as we might view it today. We need to be careful not to read our own assumptions into the text about how the world should work. However, we will see that there are issues with conscripted labour later in 1 Kings.

❓ *Does Solomon display wisdom here?*
❓ *What does the description of the workers in verses 15-18 tell us about the building of the Temple?*
❓ *How does this passage underline the importance of the temple?*

⌄ Apply

The preparations are complete. We give thanks to God with Hiram for Solomon's wisdom, and for how God has brought all these preparations together, just as he promised.

⌃ Pray

Give thanks to God for the way he keeps his promises.

A tour of the temple

The temple is built as a place to glorify God, and is a highly significant structure in both the Old and New Testaments. But what is its meaning?

The temple site

Read 1 Kings 6:1-13

- ❓ *Why do you think the narrator takes us back to the exodus here (v 1)?*
- ❓ *So what is the significance of where it stands?*

Now we read about the dimensions of the temple. The main temple is described in verse 2. We then have the porch or portico, which comes out from the front (v 3). There are also side rooms described in verses 5-6, which were constructed separately. While they were important for running the temple, we are not going to be concerned about them here. We get a little bit about them in verses 8-10, but that's it.

- ❓ *What do you think the significance of dressing the stone at the quarry was (v 7)?*

Finally we see what the temple represents in verses 11-13.

- ❓ *What does God promise about the temple?*
- ❓ *What does the warning Solomon is given imply?*

Inside the temple

Read 1 Kings 6:14-38

The temple has two parts: the main hall and the Most Holy Place (v 17-18). The Most Holy Place is a perfect cube (v 20) and is separated off from the main hall by a chain (v 21).

- ❓ *What does all the wood and carving and gold mentioned in verses 15-22 tell us about the temple?*

We then move to focus on the inner sanctuary, and we read about a pair of cherubim in verses 23-28.

- ❓ *What do all the details about the Cherubim tell us about the construction of the temple?*

Now we start to head back out of the temple, as we come to the doors, in verses 31-35. They are richly decorated with cherubim, palm trees and flowers. This links the temple back to God's creation.

We come out to the inner courtyard in front of the temple (v 36), and then are told how long the temple took to build (v 37-8).

⌃ Pray

The temple testifies to God's glory. It is the place where God will meet with his people, but at the heart of the passage is a call for obedience. Pray that you will respond to God's glory with obedience.

 Bible in a year: Daniel 11-12 • Revelation 9

Building the palaces

The focus on temple building is interrupted as we shift to Solomon's palaces. There is an implication that all is not well in the realm of the wise king.

Read 1 Kings 7:1-12

This change of focus is surprising as we will shift back to the temple in the rest of chapter 7. We might well ask—what is going on here?

> ❷ *Compare chapter 7:1 to 6:8. What does the narrator imply here?*

The first palace we read about is the Palace of the Forest of Lebanon (7:2-5). The name probably comes from the cedar pillars that made it look like a forest. It would have been an assembly hall but was also used to store gold shields (see 10:17, 21), which would have made it very impressive.

> ❷ *Compare the size of this palace with the size of the temple (6:2). What might this communicate about Solomon's priorities (7:2)?*

We read about the colonnade in 1 Kings 7:6. Because it has a portico or porch and a hanging roof, it is probably another palace—the Hall of Pillars. We then come to three further palaces in verses 7 and 8: the Hall of Justice, Solomon's palace, and palace for Pharaoh's daughter.

> ❷ *Why did Solomon need all these palaces?*

We are then told about the construction of the palaces (v 9-11). The emphasis is on the quality of the stones used, some of which were of great size. The walls around the palaces and the temple are mentioned in verse 12.

> ❷ *What is missing from the description of the palaces that is emphasised in the construction of the temple? What might this indicate?*
> ❷ *Looking at this passage as a whole, what do you think this tells us about Solomon's priorities?*

▾ Apply

This is not the first time we have considered Solomon's priorities. It is one of the things that these passages from 1 Kings encourage us to do. However, we are not just to evaluate Solomon here. We also need to look at ourselves. What are our priorities?

> ❷ *How would someone looking at our use of time and resources evaluate us? Do we put the things of God first?*

▴ Pray

Say sorry to God for the times your priorities have been wrong and pray for a heart to put the things of God first.

Two sides to the story

In today's psalm, David relates two great truths: one about man and one about God. Actually, the first truth isn't so great...

Read Psalm 36

No fear
Re-read Psalm 36:1-4

❓ *What attitude does the wicked man have towards God?*

❓ *And towards himself and his sin?*

❓ *Do you see any of these characteristics in yourself?*

The wicked think God has no bearing on their lives. They sin, thinking God won't do anything about it (v 1; see Psalm 10:11). Their self-importance (Psalm 36:2) means they suppose that they're accountable to no one but themselves (least of all God). There is no fear or reverence for the Lord. This attitude is true for many people. Even Christians, at times, live as if God is irrelevant to what they do; as if the Lord Jesus has had no impact on their lives.

Now compare this attitude with truth number two...

Life and light
Re-read Psalm 36:5-9

❓ *According to David, how is God good to his people?*

❓ *How has he shown his love and faithfulness to you particularly?*

God's love is unimaginably great (v 5). God's righteousness is shown in his perfect justice

and protection (v 6-7). He gives us life-giving food and water (v 8-9), and enables us to enjoy life in all its fullness.

···· **TIME OUT** ··

We could just see these verses as an encouragement to enjoy the wonderful gifts of food and drink—but it is so much more than that. The refrain of verses 8-9 should alert us to the way this promise is fulfilled in Jesus. These themes are brought out in John's Gospel:

• "They feast in the abundance of your house". See John 6:35.

• "Drink from your river of delights". See John 4:10-14.

• "In your light we see light". See John 1:4-9.

Two outcomes
Re-read Psalm 36:10-12

Those who never fear the Lord—who think him irrelevant—will one day be judged by him (v 12). The story is very different for those who do fear the Lord (v 8, 10).

❓ *How can you make David's prayer (v 10) your own?*

Furnishing the temple

We come back to the temple and find out more about what went inside it.

Read 1 Kings 7:13-51

In verses 13-14, we meet Huram from Tyre, a master craftsman who is part-Israelite, and we read about his work in bronze. We read first about the bronze pillars in the temple porch (v 15-22), named Jakin or "He establishes" and Boaz or "In him is strength". It is hard to know exactly what these pillars looked like, but we can get a good idea of their main features

❓ *What do you think the names and features of the pillars are telling us about the God of this temple?*

We then come to the Sea, a great basin placed in the courtyard of the temple (v 23-26), and a set of ten stands which each carried a moveable bronze basin (v 27-39). Again, the precise design of the moveable stands might escape us, but we can see the main details. Clearly the temple is going to use an enormous amount of water.

❓ *Why does the temple need all this water? What does that tell us about its purpose?*

Finally, we come to another set of items summarised in verse 40. These pots, shovels and sprinkling bowls are all tools to be used in making offerings and sacrifices. We then get a summary of all the things Huram made, using so much bronze it was not even weighed, in verses 41-47.

❓ *Why do you think we are given all this detail about the bronze work for the temple?*

We then move from bronze to gold, and to the temple interior, before the work is completed, verse 51.

❓ *What do the gold items tell us about the temple's purpose?*

···· **TIME OUT** ·······················

❓ *How does the mention of David (v 51) help us to see how God is fulfilling his promises in the building and furnishing of the temple, his "house"?*

⌄ Apply

We get a sense of the magnificence of the temple in 1 Kings 6 – 7. As we see the glory of this temple, we are reminded that it only foreshadows the coming of Jesus, who describes himself as the temple (see John 2:19-21), and who sacrificed himself for us.

⌃ Pray

Reflect on the glories of the temple described here, and then give thanks to Jesus for his death and resurrection for us.

God's glory arrives

Israel gathers as the ark enters the temple, and it seems as though the blessing and approval of God rests upon King Solomon as God's glory fills the temple.

The coming of the ark

Read 1 Kings 8:1-13

> ❓ *All Israel gathered. What have they gathered to do (v 1-6)?*

The ark of the covenant was the symbol of God's presence with Israel from the time of the exodus. In the tabernacle that Moses built it was kept in the holy of holies. The stone tablets in the ark had the Ten Commandments on them (see Exodus 20).

> ❓ *Why do you think the cherubim are mentioned again in 1 Kings 8:6-7?*
> ❓ *What do the contents of the ark tell us about how God communicates with his people?*

We see a big emphasis here on the covenant that God has made with his people, and on how God keeps his promises.

> ❓ *How do the events of verses 10-13 show us that God keeps his promises?*

Now that the ark is in the temple and the furnishing is complete, God's glory fills the temple. Just as God was with Moses and the people, and with David, so he will be with Solomon and the people.

🔼 Pray

Give thanks to God that he is a covenant God who keeps his promises.

The story so far

Read 1 Kings 8:14-21

Solomon now speaks to the people. He reminds them of the promises that God has made, and the promises that God has kept. For more than 400 years, God didn't choose a place to put the temple, but he has chosen David, verse 16. Solomon is the one who will build the temple, verses 17-19. And this has now come to pass.

> ❓ *Why do you think that Solomon goes over what has just happened?*
> ❓ *Twice Solomon mentions the exodus from Egypt, in verses 16 and 21. How does this reinforce Solomon's point?*

☑ Apply

Solomon carefully goes through what God has promised, and what God has done. We can follow his example, in reminding ourselves of all the promises God has made, whether to Moses, or David, or Solomon, or in Jesus, and reflect on how he has kept them.

And so, we can praise him for keeping his promises, and have confidence that he will keep all the promises he has made us in Jesus.

Solomon's prayer

At the dedication of the temple, Solomon prays that God will keep his promises.

Read 1 Kings 8:22-53

Solomon has just blessed the people (v 14-21). Now he prays to God.

❓ *What is the significance of the details we are given about the prayer in verse 22?*

❓ *What is the basis for Solomon's prayer that God will keep his promises made to David in verses 23-26?*

Solomon prays before the altar with confidence that God will keep his promises to David. But he knows that God doesn't dwell in the temple.

❓ *Why is Solomon confident that God will hear prayers made towards the temple (v 27-30)?*

Solomon then goes through a series of situations that might happen in years to come (v 31-53). In each case, Solomon prays that God will hear from heaven and act. For example, in verse 32, God is to hear and act and judge between the guilty and the innocent.

We then see situations of military defeat (v 33-34), drought (v 35-36), and other disasters (v 37-40)

❓ *Why do these things happen, and what do the people need to do?*

We then meet the foreigner who has come to find out more about God (v 41-43) and we hear a prayer for victory in battle (v 44-45); two contrasting responses from non-Israelites.

❓ *How should the nations be responding to God?*

Finally, we come to the situation where God's people face exile for rebellion against God, verse 46. Solomon knows that the people are sinful. He knows that God will ultimately punish them by throwing them out of the land if they continue to rebel against him.

❓ *What should the people do when they find themselves in exile (v 47-48)?*

❓ *Why should God be merciful to the people (v 49-53)?*

⌄ Apply

Solomon's prayer is realistic and prophetic. He knows what the people are like. After all, they have consistently rebelled against God from Egypt onwards. He knows that God is just and will hold his people to account. But he also knows that God is merciful and will hear the prayers of his people if they truly repent. Solomon's realism encourages us to be realistic about our sins, and to come in true repentance to God, seeking his mercy.

⌃ Pray

Say sorry to God for the sins that burden you, confident of his forgiveness in Jesus Christ.

Promises and warnings

Solomon blesses the people, the temple is dedicated, and God then speaks to Solomon. It is a time of opportunity, and of challenge.

Dedication

Read 1 Kings 8:54-66

Having finished his prayer, Solomon rises to bless the people. He praises God for his faithfulness, and then asks for four more things of God on behalf of the people in verses 56 to 61.

❷ *What does Solomon ask of God?*
❷ *Why is this important?*
❷ *How should the people respond to God?*

We then come to the dedication of the temple. The number of offerings and sacrifices are huge—so huge that they have to be made in the courtyard (v 62-64). The festival is observed in verses 65-66, from Lebo Hamath in the north to the Wadi of Egypt in the south. This is the Feast of Tabernacles or Booths (Deuteronomy 16:13-15), a time when God's people gathered to give thanks for the harvest. The celebrations last 14 days, before the people go home rejoicing.

❷ *What was the atmosphere like in Israel at the time the temple was dedicated?*

✅ Apply

This was the best of times; a time of promises fulfilled and great blessings. We can follow the Israelites' example here in rejoicing for the good things God gives us.

Dedicated to the Lord?

Read 1 Kings 9:1-9

God appears to Solomon a second time in a dream as at Gibeon.

❷ *Who has consecrated the temple (v 3)?*
❷ *What does God promise Solomon, and what does Solomon need to do (v 4-5)?*
❷ *What will happen if the people turn away from God (v 6-9)?*

After the high point of the end of chapter 8, these verses are a bit of a reality check. God is with his people, but Solomon needs to lead the people *to* God, not *away* from God to other gods. After all, why would a people forsake the God who rescued them from Egypt (9:9)?

✅ Apply

Our circumstances are different, but the issue of faithfulness to God remains. Jesus calls us to follow him wholeheartedly, and not to be distracted by the things of this world.

▲ Pray

Pray that God will help you to follow Jesus faithfully.

What kind of king?

As the narrator tells us some more of the things that Solomon did, we discover what kind of king he was .

Read 1 Kings 9:10-28

Building the temple and palaces has taken Solomon 20 years (v 10), and so we now move into the second half of his reign. We are told a number of things that Solomon did. What do you make of them?

In verses 11-14, we learn of Solomon's dealings with Hiram, his ally in Tyre and Sidon.

❷ *What do you make of how Solomon treats his "brother" Hiram?*

Then we come to the forced labour. This labour wasn't just for the temple, but for lots of other building work as well (v 15-19).

❷ *What impression does this passage give of Solomon's priorities as king?*

The mention of towns for chariots and horses in verse 19 is significant as it reminds us that Solomon was a powerful king. However, it also reminds us of the warnings given earlier in the Bible, in 1 Samuel 8 where Samuel the prophet warns Israel that a king will have many chariots and make the people his servants and even slaves. Is this the very thing that Samuel warned of?

···· **TIME OUT** ·····································

As well as the passage in 1 Samuel 8, Moses addresses similar issues in Deuteronomy 17:14-20 about what a king should and should not do.

❷ *How does Solomon measure up to these standards?*

We then come to the descendants of the people the Israelites failed to "exterminate" (1 Kings 9:20-23). The narrator reminds us of the specific instructions given to Joshua and his generation to act as God's agents of judgment when they conquered the land.

❷ *What does the narrator want us to know about the difference between Israelites and non-Israelites?*
❷ *What picture of the king do we get from what is reported in verses 24-28?*

⌄ Apply

This is another opportunity to evaluate Solomon.

❷ *What do you make of him?*
❷ *How might his strengths and weaknesses help you to evaluate yourself?*

⌃ Pray

Pray that you would have a right understanding of yourself and be able to say sorry for the times when you have not been faithful to God. Pray that you would serve God faithfully with the gifts you have.

Coming to the king

We now see all the glories of Solomon, seen in his international reputation for wealth and wisdom.

The queen comes

Read 1 Kings 10:1-13

❷ *What happens when the queen of Sheba arrives in verses 1-5?*
❷ *Why did she come (v 1, 6-7)?*
❷ *What is her response to Solomon in verses 8-10?*

The queen of Sheba comes in all her glory and sees the greater glory of Solomon. She gives Solomon gifts, although, as the narrator points out in verses 11-12, Solomon has many other sources of wealth. And Solomon returns the favour (v 13).

⌄ Apply

The queen comes to Solomon and receives all that she desires. Solomon, as David's son, is a picture for us of King David's greater son, Jesus. Solomon's great glory points us to the even greater glory that is in Jesus. How much more will all who come to Jesus the King receive all that they desire?

⌃ Pray

Pray for a greater sense of all that we receive in Jesus.

The splendour of the king

Read 1 Kings 10:14-29

❷ *How does the narrator emphasise Solomon's wealth?*
❷ *How is Solomon's power emphasised?*

We are reminded of Solomon's wisdom (v 23-25), which drew not just the queen of Sheba but people from many nations along with their gifts.

❷ *What is it that the people come to hear?*

Finally, we come to a section about chariots and horses in verses 26-29. Solomon's wealth is emphasised, as well as the wealth of the people in Jerusalem (v 27). He is a successful trader in horseflesh, no doubt because he controlled the trade routes north and south.

❷ *How does this section back up what we already know about Solomon?*

⌄ Apply

This chapter makes it very clear that Solomon's reign was glorious, the king was very rich, very wise, and drew people to Israel to hear about God. These were glorious times. But all the glories of Solomon were temporary. Just as Solomon points us to Jesus, so his temporary glories point us to the permanent glories of Jesus, our greater King.

⌃ Pray

Praise Jesus Christ, our glorious King.

The wicked v the righteous

In Psalm 37, David touches on an area that Christians sometimes struggle with: how is it that the wicked often seem to prosper, while the godly suffer?

Don't get sucked in

Read Psalm 37:1-9

❷ *Why should we not fret or be anxious about nor envious of the wicked?*
❷ *Are you currently experiencing any of these feelings now? Against whom?*
❷ *What should you do with those feelings, according to these verses?*

It's true, often the godless do well in this world (v 7), while the godly face trials and temptations. But just look at David's wonderful advice and encouragement! Don't worry about it or get jealous (v 1), because the success of the wicked won't last (v 2)! We are to trust the Lord, do good (v 3) and enjoy safe pasture (or "befriend faithfulness", ESV). Our delight should be in the Lord (not the sinful pleasures of this life), for he gives us all we need and desire (v 4). We are to be patient, even when the godless seem to prevail (v 7). For God will make our righteousness (the fact that we're in the right with God) shine like the rising sun (v 6).

❷ *Which piece of advice in verses 1-9 is particularly relevant to you right now?*
❷ *What will you do to put it into action?*

Eternal differences

Read Psalm 37:10-22

❷ *What additional perspective on this question does David now think about?*

❷ *Why do we find this difficult to hold onto at times?*
❷ *Do you truly believe verse 16—be honest!*

The contrast continues. The prosperity of the wicked will not last; they will be wiped from the face of the earth (v 10). Eternally, their schemes will come to nothing. Their opposition to God's people can be terrible (v 12, 14) and can really get us down. But God laughs at the wicked (v 13), because he has already sealed their fate. Their power will be broken (v 17), they will perish (v 20), and be cut off from God for ever (v 22).

❷ *What, by contrast, will become of the poor, despised servants of the Lord?*

For God's people, the future couldn't possibly look brighter! Those who depend on him will receive their inheritance. An inheritance that will last eternally. And that future is so certain, that they can count themselves wealthier than the wicked already (v 16).

❷ *From today's psalm, which piece of encouragement is most important for you right now?*

▲ Pray

Pray for the person or regime you thought about at the start of this study.

And pray for yourself, and those who are being persecuted by wicked people. Ask the Lord to fill them with the reassurance that this psalm gives.

Solomon's fall

Solomon's glorious reign comes to a tragic end because of the sin that had been lurking for so long beneath the gilded splendour of his reign.

Solomon's sin

Read 1 Kings 11:1-13

- ❓ *Why are Solomon's foreign wives a problem in verses 1-5?*
- ❓ *Why do you think the narrator includes a comparison to David here (v 6)?*

Solomon not only built a temple to the Lord; he also builds places of sacrifice to other gods (v 7-8). So, God is justly angry with Solomon, and will punish him (v 9-11).

- ❓ *How does the punishment fit the crime?*
- ❓ *What hope does God give for the future, and why (v 12-13)?*

Solomon was led astray and followed other gods or idols. No doubt Solomon still worshipped God in the temple, but he no longer worshipped only God.

⌄ Apply

We too have things in our lives that lead us away from wholeheartedly seeking God, even though we would say we are still following Jesus. Our idols are not made of stone or wood, and are more likely to be things like pleasure, money, power and status, leisure activities, educational achievements, our families, or our own bodies. These things are good gifts of God, but not a suitable replacement for God.

- ❓ *What kinds of things might lead us away from Jesus?*

⌃ Pray

Ask God to show you the things of this life that you might be tempted to make more important than Jesus.

Ask God to help you to enjoy the good gifts of this life with thankfulness and contentment.

Hadad the Edomite

Read 1 Kings 11:14-22

- ❓ *Why would Hadad be an enemy of Solomon?*
- ❓ *Why do you think Pharaoh would support Hadad?*
- ❓ *Why does Hadad return to Edom?*

⌄ Apply

Hadad's opposition to Solomon is easy to understand, and we can see why, humanly speaking, these events happen. But we are also told in verse 14 that God raises Hadad up as an enemy to Solomon. We are reminded that God works through ordinary events as well as extraordinary events to bring about his plans and purposes. As we see the tragedy of Solomon's fall, it is good to remember that God is in charge.

⌃ Pray

Give thanks that God is always at work, bringing about his plans and purposes.

Solomon's end

The kingdom that had been secure and glorious for so many years under Solomon starts to fall apart as he nears his end.

Read 1 Kings 11:23-43

❓ *Why does Rezon oppose Solomon (v 23-25)?*

Previously we met Hadad—Solomon's enemy to the south (Edom). Now we meet Rezon, Solomon's enemy in Aram, a kingdom to the north-west of Israel. Pharaoh also appears less friendly, so we see that Solomon has enemies all around. But worse is to come.

❓ *How does Jeroboam become an important person in Israel (v 26-28)?*

Jeroboam is over the forced labour for the tribes of Joseph (Ephraim and Manasseh). He is a reminder of the power of those northern tribes, and that Solomon used forced labour.

We then meet Ahijah, a prophet from Shiloh. Shiloh was the place where the tabernacle was based before the temple was built in Jerusalem. Here we see the emergence of prophets who are not members of the king's court, but who operate independently, calling Israel and her kings back to God.

❓ *Why do you think Ahijah tears his cloak as well as delivering God's message?*

Ahijah delivers a fuller version of the message God has already given Solomon. All but one tribe will be lost to Solomon's descendants.

❓ *How does Ahijah describe what it means to follow God (v 33)?*

❓ *Why is it important that God has "a lamp ... in Jerusalem" (v 36)?*

Ahijah's word is not just one of judgment; he also makes promises to Jeroboam in verses 37 to 39.

❓ *What does Jeroboam need to do?*

⌄ Apply

In these verses we see the pattern of what it means to follow God. We see the call to obedience, but we see that this call to obedience is based on God's promises, and God always keeps his promises. We can remind ourselves of the promises God has made us in Jesus: how he lived, died, and rose again for us, and then seek to follow him.

⌃ Pray

Recall and give thanks to God for all that he has done for you in Jesus. Ask for a heart to obey his word.

Finally, in verses 41-43, we come to Solomon's death. We are reminded of the good things of Solomon: his wisdom and his long reign, and that he was buried and followed on the throne by his son.

⌄ Apply

❓ *We have spent eleven chapters with Solomon. What do you most need to learn from this part of God's word?*

Rehoboam's folly

Solomon's son Rehoboam comes to the throne. What kind of king will he be?

A hard king
Read 1 Kings 12:1-15

We begin chapter 12 with a united kingdom. All Israel comes to Shechem to make Rehoboam king. But Jeroboam is also there (v 2-3).

> ❷ *What do the people want from their king (v 2-4)?*

Rehoboam takes advice. First from the elders (v 6-7), and then from the young men he grew up with (v 9-11). Their advice is very different to the elders.

> ❷ *Why do you think Rehoboam preferred the advice of the young men?*

The people return to receive their answer in verse 12.

> ❷ *What does the narrator think about Rehoboam's response (v 13-14)?*
> ❷ *What else is going on here (v 15)?*

☑ Apply

Rehoboam gives the answer he prefers. He wants to be the "big man", the strong leader. And yet at the same time, God is at work in this decision to bring about his purposes. Rehoboam's decision is unwise, and yet God is at work through it. We can take comfort that God is achieving his purposes, even when his people and their leaders are acting unwisely.

A divided kingdom
Read 1 Kings 12:16-24

> ❷ *Why do you think the kingdom divides as it does in verses 16-17?*
> ❷ *What happens to make the division permanent (v 18-20)?*

···· **TIME OUT** ····

The early chapters of 2 Samuel show a similar distinction between Judah and Israel. There are two kings in 2 Samuel 2:1-11, and there is a war before David becomes king over Israel in 2 Samuel 5.

Rehoboam musters his forces to get back his kingdom in verse 21. Then the prophet Shemaiah comes to tell Judah not to fight against the Israelites in verses 22-24. Perhaps surprisingly, the people hear and obey the word of the Lord.

The kingdom is divided, and the people are divided; not only between Israel and Judah, but also in their response to God. Sometimes the king and the people listen, sometimes they don't. This divided loyalty plays a big part in the eventual downfall of the kingdom.

☑ Pray

Pray for a heart to rightly respond to God when we hear him through his word.

 Bible in a year: Numbers 17-19 • Revelation 21

Jeroboam's folly

The scene shifts to the northern kingdom, and we see what kind of king Jeroboam really is.

Golden calves

Read 1 Kings 12:25-33

❓ *What is Jeroboam worried about in verses 25-27?*

Jeroboam decides he needs an alternative worship centre in the north. He sets up golden calves—idols—in the north of his kingdom (Dan) and in the south (Bethel) in verses 28-30. He sets up his own priest-hood, and his own festivals in verses 31-33.

❓ *What is the problem with Jeroboam's actions in verses 28-33?*

···· TIME OUT ····························

Read Exodus 34:1-10. How does this passage help us to see what a big problem the golden calves were?

⌄ Apply

The narrator makes it very clear what he thinks about the calves (1 Kings 12:30), Jeroboam's priests (v 31) and his made-up festival. Jeroboam did these things for understandable human reasons: to protect his kingdom, but that does not excuse the breaking of the first two commandments. We can all be driven by this kind of idolatry, which is ultimately a failure of trust in God's promises.

❓ *Where might we be tempted to act like Jeroboam?*

A strange encounter

Read 1 Kings 13:1-10

We begin this chapter with Jeroboam at the altar in Bethel. A man of God comes to confront him (v 1).

❓ *What message does he bring? How will it be authenticated (v 2-3)?*

We won't come across Josiah until 2 Kings 22, around 300 years after the events here.

❓ *Why should we believe this messenger (1 Kings 13:4-5)?*

Jeroboam initially wants the man seized in verse 4, but as his hand shrivels so does his pride, and he asks for and receives restoration and then offers hospitality.

❓ *Why do you think the man of God was given these strange instructions (v 8-10)?*

⌄ Apply

The man of God faithfully delivers God's message of what is going to happen in 300 years. God's purposes are set even when things look like they are going in the wrong direction as in the last few chapters of 1 Kings—or in our own lives.

⌃ Pray

Give thanks to God that he is in charge in all circumstances and pray for confidence in him in the midst of challenging times.

Bible in a year: Numbers 20-22 • Revelation 22 ⌄

Two prophets

We continue the story of the unnamed man of God, which comes to a surprising end.

Read 1 Kings 13:11-34

Having met the man of God from Judah yesterday, we meet an old prophet from Bethel today. This is a strange story, so let's follow it through before we reflect on what it means for us.

❷ *What are our first impressions of the old prophet (v 11-15)?*

The prophet invites the man of God for a meal, which he naturally refuses, given what God has told him (v 15-17). But the old prophet is insistent.

❷ *What persuades the man of God to go with the old prophet (v 18-19)?*

Now God speaks through the old prophet. The man of God has been disobedient to God, and so he will not be buried in the tomb of his ancestors. We'll see what this means shortly. And so, he continues his journey (v 23).

❷ *What has the man of God failed to do?*
❷ *What is strange about how the lion behaves (v 24-25)?*

The old prophet confirms in verse 26 that this has happened as the Lord promised.

❷ *Why do you think the old prophet acts as he does in verses 27-30?*
❷ *Why does the old prophet want to share a grave with the man of God (v 31-32)?*
❷ *What is Jeroboam's response to all this in verses 33-34?*

☑ Apply

In many ways this is one of the strangest passages in 1 Kings—if not in the whole Bible. We meet two prophets but aren't told the name of either. One faithfully and courageously delivers God's message to Jeroboam but is killed by God for disobeying his word about eating and drinking.

The other deceives the faithful messenger, but then mourns his death and confirms the truth of his word. We are dealing here with the issue of true and false prophecy, as to whether everything that people claim comes from God can be believed, however plausible the messenger is. It is a really important question that has faced God's people throughout the ages.

❷ *How can we make sure that we are only hearing true words from God?*
❷ *How does this passage challenge us to respond to those who claim to come with a word to us from God?*

☒ Pray

Pray for wisdom to rightly understand God's word as we read it alone and study it with others.

Pray for discernment among God's people about the leaders they listen to and the messages they embrace.

The end of Jeroboam

We come to the end of Jeroboam's reign, but there is also a greater end to come.

Read 1 Kings 14:1-20

Jeroboam has a problem. His son is ill, hard for any parent, but doubly so for a king. If his son dies, who will reign after him? So, he sends his wife with a gift to enquire of Ahijah the prophet in verses 1-3.

❷ *Why do you think Jeroboam sends his wife in disguise?*

Even though he can't see, God reveals to Ahijah that Jeroboam's wife is coming (v 4-5). He has bad news for her.

❷ *What reason is given in verses 7-9 for the bad news that Jeroboam will receive?*

Jeroboam has sent his wife to find out what will happen to their son. Ahijah tells them what will happen to the whole family of Jeroboam in verses 10-11. They will be wiped out and won't even receive a proper burial.

❷ *How is what happens to Abijah related to God finding good in him (v 12-13)?*

God will appoint a new king over Israel to replace Jeroboam (v 14), just as Jeroboam was appointed by God over the northern kingdom which God took from Rehoboam. We can see a clear pattern emerging here of how God punishes the sin of his people. However, there is more here in verses 15-16.

❷ *What will happen to Israel if they keep on sinning and making idols?*

Jeroboam's wife returns home, and her son dies and is mourned, just as Ahijah promised (v 17-18). We then get a brief notice about the end of Jeroboam's reign in verses 19 and 20.

❷ *Why is this partial fulfilment of Ahijah's prophecy (Abijah's death) important?*

❷ *What might the summary of Jeroboam's reign tell us about what the author of Kings is interested in?*

⌄ Apply

Jeroboam's reign comes to an end. What began as a new start after the sin of Solomon comes to an end with the northern kingdom firmly established in false worship (see 12:25-33). Despite prophetic warnings, the king is unrepentant (13:1-10). So, Jeroboam's dynasty will end, and so will Israel's if she also doesn't repent (14:15-16).

❷ *How does this passage challenge us to take seriously God's condemnation of idolatry and false worship?*

❷ *What forms of idolatry do you think are particularly tempting for Christians in your church today?*

Bible in a year: Numbers 26-28 • Matthew 2

True prosperity

In the first half of Psalm 37, David compared the wicked with the righteous. The wicked often prosper and succeed in their schemes, but God will wipe them out.

God's people—the righteous—suffer in this life. They are warned against jealousy (v 1) and impatience (v 7) and promised that they will receive an eternal inheritance from the Lord (v 18). In today's passage there's more of the same from David. But it's your turn to do the hard work...

Read Psalm 37:23-38

❷ *Which description of the wicked particularly strikes you?*

Write it out here:

Now use it to pray for people you know who are rejecting God.

❷ *Which verse challenges you to change the way you live?*

Write it out here:

Now pray about how you will seek to make that change happen—with the help of God's Spirit and his people.

❷ *Which verse encourages you, as you strive to live for the Lord?*

Write it out here:

Now share this thought with another believer you meet or talk with today. Perhaps pause now to text a friend with what has encouraged you.

⌃ Pray

Read verses 39-40 and turn them into a prayer of praise and thanksgiving to our awesome Father in heaven.

Three kings of Judah

The scene shifts to the southern kingdom—Judah—and her first three kings. At first, it seems as disastrous and hopeless as the north. But there are glimmers of hope…

Two bad kings
Read 1 Kings 14:21 – 15:8

We have met Rehoboam before in 1 Kings 12, but here we get a summary of his reign which sets a pattern for how kings are described in the rest of the book: beginning (14:21), evaluation of acts (v 22-28), end of reign (v 29-31).

❷ *How did Judah do evil (v 22-24)?*

Given what we have seen so far, it is no surprise that Shishak comes up from Egypt to plunder the temple and palace in verses 25 and 26. Rehoboam's guards are reduced to carrying bronze shields (v 27-28).

We end with a reference to other acts, to war, to burial, and to Rehoboam's son in verses 29-31. This is a standard pattern, and it is worth noticing when it varies from the usual pattern.

❷ *Why do you think Rehoboam's mother is mentioned twice (v 21, 31)?*

We then meet Abijah (or Abijam, ESV).

❷ *What kind of king was Abijah (v 1-3)?*
❷ *Why wasn't Abijah treated as his sins deserved (v 4-5)?*

We come to the end of Abijah's brief reign in verses 6-8. Judah is no better than the northern kingdom, yet God remains faithful to his promise to David despite the idolatry and corruption of his people and their leader.

One good king
Read 1 Kings 15:9-24

Asa's reign lasts for 41 years and will cover all the kings of the northern kingdom we will come to next.

❷ *What is positive about Asa's reign?*

Asa is at war with Baasha who is a significant threat to Judah (v 16) and so Asa makes an alliance with Ben-Hadad in Damascus, to the north-east of Israel. Ben-Hadad attacks, and forces Baasha to withdraw (v 20-22).

❷ *Asa's strategy works. But how wise was it to rely on a foreign power?*

···· TIME OUT ································

Read 2 Chronicles 16:7-10 for a further analysis of what Asa did here.

⌄ Apply

Judah is still God's favoured kingdom, but its kings are far from perfect, even the good ones. As we see the continual failure of human kings, we recognise our need for a true son of David.

⌃ Pray

Give thanks that we have in Jesus the perfect King on whom we can wholly rely.

Five and a half kings

While Judah has a period of relative stability under a good but imperfect king (Asa), back in the northern kingdom of Israel we meet a long line of godless men.

New men, same problems

Read 1 Kings 15:25 – 16:7

Our first king is Jeroboam's son Nadab.

❓ *Why was Nadab struck down (15:25-30)?*

Nadab's brief reign comes to an end, and then we meet his assassin and next king, Baasha. Sadly, it is just more of the same.

❓ *What does the prophecy in 16:1-4 tell us about how God deals with the kings of Israel?*

Baasha reigned for 24 years, and clearly had some achievements (v 5-6). However, as with all the kings, the narrator is concerned less with his human accomplishments and more with his spiritual state—whether he led his people to or away from God.

❓ *How does verse 7 emphasise the seriousness of Baasha's sin?*

There is grace in being given a prophetic warning, but also a pattern of God's just judgment on continued rebellion against him. That pattern continues.

Chaos reigns

Read 1 Kings 16:8-28

Elah's reign is told very briefly with a focus on Zimri.

❓ *How does Elah's death tell us about what kind of king he was (v 9-10)?*

❓ *God's anger is aroused here. Why is God so angry about idolatry (v 11-13)?*

Zimri is our fourth king. But the army prefers Omri and fights Zimri, who kills himself and burns down the royal palace (v 18).

❓ *What reasons are we given for Zimri's death in verses 16-19?*

Our fifth king is Omri, although half of the people support Tibni for king (v 21-28). When Omri becomes king Israel is in chaos. He has to contend with a rival king, then he builds a new capital, Samaria, in a strategic place (v 24). In many ways he brought stability to Israel.

❓ *How does the evaluation of Omri in verses 25-28 help you understand what is important?*

⌄ Apply

In the midst of the chaos and godlessness of these chapters, we continue to see God's sovereign hand at work, achieving his purposes, even through men like Baasha, Zimri and Omri. As we face chaotic situations in our lives—at work, in our families, or even at church—give thanks that God is still in charge.

And know too that in a chaotic, changing world with "wars and rumours of wars" all around, the Lord still reigns, and the same things remain important—faithfulness to the Lord.

✔ *Bible in a year: Numbers 35-36 • Matthew 5 v 1-26*

Ahab and Elijah

Now we are introduced to the worst king, as well as the great prophet. The clash between them is so much more than a church/state power struggle.

Bad King Ahab

Read 1 Kings 16:29-34

We are still in the reign of Asa in the south when Ahab becomes king of the north (v 29).

❓ *Why is Ahab such a bad king (v 30-33)?*

The Israelites have had problems with Baal before, back in the time of the judges. Baal was a storm god, worshipped by the Phoenicians in places like Tyre and Sidon, and also by the Canaanites. Asherah was a mother-goddess, and Baal's consort. Together they represented fertility, and Baal was in charge of the rain.

❓ *What does the founding of Jericho tell us about what Israel was like at this time (see also Joshua 6:26)?*

Apply

Israel has moved from false worship of God using idols, to worship of false gods—the Baal and the Asherah. We can see how this might have helped secure an alliance with Tyre and Sidon, and helps Ahab in his relations with his wife, Jezebel. We can also imagine the pragmatic reasons why going to the temple of a god who promises rain might be attractive. Putting our trust in things other than God is tempting, and often has a powerful rationale to it.

❓ *What reasons might we give ourselves to put our trust in things other than God?*

▲ Pray

Pray for wisdom to understand and reject the false arguments we make to ourselves— and so resist these temptations.

Elijah appears

Read 1 Kings 17:1-6

Elijah appears from an obscure place, but with a clear message for Ahab (v 1).

❓ *What is the hope that Elijah offers?*

Drought is one of the punishments that Israel will suffer for rebelling against God. In 8:35-6, we read what the response of the people should be: repentance and seeking the Lord. We don't see any of that here.

❓ *Why do you think God commands Elijah to effectively hide in 17:3?*

Having delivered his message, Elijah withdraws, and is fed by God in the wilderness (v 4-6).

Apply

Elijah is God's prophet, who speaks God's word. God's messenger is provided for, but Israel is under God's judgment. When God speaks, his people must listen

❓ *How can you ensure that you are ready to listen to God's word?*

God patiently provides

In the middle of a nationwide drought and famine, God provides for his servant Elijah, and also for a surprising family.

Read 1 Kings 17:7-24

Ahab and Israel are under God's judgement for worshipping Baal and Asherah, and there is no rain (v 7). But God is still speaking to Elijah and sends him to the region of Sidon, into the heart of "Baal territory".

❓ *Why is it surprising that Elijah is sent into Sidon, not Israel, for help?*
❓ *Why is the widow an unlikely source of help?*
❓ *What does Elijah discover when he asks the widow for help (v 10-12)?*
❓ *Why can Elijah tell the widow with such confidence not to be afraid (v 13-16)?*

God works miraculously in the life of this widow, but then it all goes horribly wrong.

❓ *Why does the widow blame Elijah's presence for her son's death in verse 18?*
❓ *What does Elijah's prayer tell us about his relationship with God (v 19-21)?*

God again works miraculously in the life of this widow, by raising her son to life.

❓ *What does the widow's response in verse 24 teach us about Elijah's miracles?*

···· TIME OUT ·······································

Jesus refers to this incident in **Luke 4:24-30**, when the people of Nazareth are rejecting him because he is Joseph's son.

❓ *What does Jesus teach about why Elijah was sent to Zarephath?*

Elijah has already pronounced a God-ordained drought and been miraculously fed by God in the wilderness (1 Kings 17:1-7). But here we see the first and second of a number of miracles that Elijah does. These kinds of miracles don't happen very often in the Bible and point us to how important Elijah is as a prophet. This is reinforced by passages such as Malachi 4:4-6 and Mark 9:4 which link Elijah and Moses as the representative Old Testament prophets.

⌄ Apply

Elijah brings God's word to Israel despite the rebellion of her kings and people. Israel's kings have consistently rejected God and turned to idols, and yet God still sends his prophet.

❓ *What does this teach us about how God deals with his rebellious people?*
❓ *Elijah's miracles remind us of some of the things that Jesus did. How else does Elijah point you to Jesus here?*
❓ *Elijah goes to Sidon, not Israel, and works miracles. What does this teach you about God's grace?*

⌃ Pray

Give thanks for God's patience with his people, and his grace towards us—even when we are cold-hearted and rebellious.

God v Baal

The scene is set for a major showdown, with Elijah seemingly alone against the king, his prophets and the people. But in this kind of contest, there is only one winner.

Elijah and Obadiah

Read 1 Kings 18:1-18

God sends Elijah to Ahab, who is hunting for Elijah.

> ❷ What does Ahab's concern in verse 5 tell us about his priorities?
> ❷ Why is Obadiah reluctant to tell Ahab that Elijah has come (v 9-14)?

This time, Elijah comes to meet Ahab, who accuses Elijah of troubling Israel (v 17) because of the drought. But it is Ahab who is really responsible for the drought (v 18).

⌄ Apply

Obadiah worked for Ahab but used his position to save the prophets (v 4, 13). He served faithfully in a difficult position.

> ❷ How might his example give you confidence to serve in difficult circumstances?

An uneven contest

Read 1 Kings 18:19-46

There is to be a contest at Mount Carmel (v 19-20).

> ❷ What is the contest really about (v 21)?
> ❷ The prophets cry out, and Elijah mocks them (v 25-29). What does the narrator emphasise (v 29)?

> ❷ Elijah's turn comes. Why does he rebuild the altar in verses 31-32?
> ❷ Why does Elijah soak the bull (v 32-35)?
> ❷ What does Elijah's prayer reveal about the purpose of this contest (v 36-39)?

In dramatic fashion, God reveals himself as Lord, and the people respond; the prophets of Baal are judged. Having demonstrated his power, God will now send rain. It takes a while for the rain to come while Elijah prays. God operates to his own time schedule.

> ❷ Elijah twice gives Ahab instructions here, and Ahab obeys. What might this suggest about Ahab's character?

Ahab goes to Jezreel by chariot, but Elijah travels by the hand of the Lord and reaches Jezreel first. He goes before Ahab, probably indicating that Ahab should continue to listen to God's messenger, as he has done briefly here.

⌃ Pray

God reveals his power, and this leads to judgment of those opposed to God. However, there is also grace for the people and for Ahab, who is again offered the opportunity to listen to God's word.

Thank God for his undeserved grace to you. And pray that you would have a firm resolve to follow Christ and not waver between two opinions.

After the ordeal

The Lord has shown his power in a dramatic, unambiguous and decisive way. But how will Ahab and the people respond in the longer term?

Read 1 Kings 19:1-21

❓ *What does Jezebel's response to Elijah's actions tell us (v 1-2)?*

The word translated "afraid" (v 3) is probably better translated with the more neutral "saw": Elijah saw Jezebel's response, was discouraged, and fled into the wilderness.

❓ *How does God answer Elijah's request to die in verses 5-8?*

God brings Elijah to Mount Horeb, the mountain of God. This is the place where God met with Moses and the people in Exodus. It is also called Mount Sinai. It is the place where God will meet with Elijah.

❓ *Why has Elijah come to Mount Horeb (v 10)?*
❓ *God reveals himself to Elijah in a gentle whisper (v 11-12). Why do you think God reveals himself to Elijah in this way?*

Elijah hears and comes out to meet with God, who repeats his question from verse 9. Elijah's response in verse 14 is the same: God's people have rejected the covenant, so what now?

❓ *How does God's response to Elijah in verses 15-18 answer the issues that Elijah raises in verses 10 and 14?*

These verses tell us what is going to happen next in 1 and 2 Kings. We won't meet Jehu until 2 Kings 9, but he will judge Ahab's house in 2 Kings 9 and 10. Hazael we will meet in 2 Kings 8, and he too will be God's agent of judgment on Israel. We meet Elisha in the next verse.

❓ *Elisha is a prophet like Elijah. What is surprising about how his ministry is described in 1 Kings 19:17?*

Elijah is obedient to God and finds Elisha. He throws his cloak around him to appoint him as his successor (v 19).

❓ *How do Elisha's actions in verses 20-21 show that he has left his old life behind to serve Elijah?*

⌄ Apply

God's people have failed to respond to God's word, and so the prophet feels things are hopeless; he is crushed. But God reassures him that there are still people who are faithful to the Lord and there is a plan for the future. God provides a companion and successor to the work that must continue.

⌃ Pray

Give thanks to God that, even when things look hopeless, he is still in control, and will preserve his faithful people through Jesus Christ.

Pray that you, and everyone you know involved in ministry would persevere even through crushing disappointment.

In the sin bin

How do we view ourselves as Christians? We know two things: we are utterly sinful, and we are utterly forgiven through the death of the Lord Jesus for us.

Holding the two thoughts together can be difficult sometimes, but this psalm will help.

Under God's wrath

Read Psalm 38:1-11

> ❓ *What is David terrified about (v 1-2)?*
> ❓ *Why would this be so serious (v 3-4)?*

David is brutal in the way he sees himself—the sickness of sin penetrates to his very core. He is infested with its disease (v 3); drowning in its ocean (v 4); rotting from its poison (v 5); deeply depressed by its implications (v 6); and crushed by its terrible weight upon him (v 8).

Approaching God's throne

Read Psalm 38:12-17

The mark of the true believer is this: not only can they look honestly inside themselves and see what they truly are but that knowledge draws them to God, who has mercy enough to forgive them.

> ❓ *What does David do when he is at his lowest point (v 15)?*

Seeking forgiveness

Read Psalm 38:18-22

He doesn't wallow in his sin, indulging himself in self-pity. He doesn't hang onto sin, because, deep down, he'd really like to do it

again. And he doesn't pretend that his sin hasn't spoiled his relationship with God. He lays it before God in all its ugly reality—and leaves it there!

> ❓ *What makes him so confident he can do this (v 21-22)?*

How different from many of us! Do we treat our past sin as something to smile about, or even half fondly remember as the wild times of our youth? And our current sins as mere "interesting character traits" that God will forgive, because that's his job? Perhaps we need to rediscover what real grieving over our sin is—because his Spirit within us is grieved by it; and our Father is so incensed by it that his blazing wrath is kindled.

☑ Apply

We may be utterly dejected and ashamed. But at the same time we are supremely confident in the God who forgives through the cross of Christ.

It's hard to hold together, but that is the way that believers should think of themselves.

> ❓ *Is that how you think of yourself?*

︿ Pray

Spend some time on your knees (why not literally?) before our holy, awesome God in both confession and joy.

God, Samaria and Aram

God gives Ahab a great victory, but Ahab's character runs true to form—and the result is not a victory for God's people, despite being victorious on the field.

A great victory

Read 1 Kings 20:1-34

Samaria is under attack. Things are desperate, and Ahab is willing to agree to be subject to the king of Aram.

> ❷ *But why won't Ahab agree to Ben-Hadad's further demands (v 5-9)?*

The two kings engage in a war of words (v 10-11) before the actual fighting starts. Ben-Hadad's confidence suggests he has the upper hand. But God sends a prophet to tell Ahab how to win the battle.

> ❷ *How does Ahab respond to the prophetic word in verses 15-17?*

Ben-Hadad's confidence has turned to overconfidence in verses 17 and 18. He doesn't take the attack seriously. The battle goes just as the prophet promised it would, and the Arameans are routed. But this is not over—there will be war again the next year.

> ❷ *What does the advice the officials give the king of Aram reveal about their understanding of "the gods" (v 23-25)?*

The armies muster again, and the Israelite army is much smaller.

> ❷ *What does the victory that God grants here demonstrate (v 28-30)?*

Ben-Hadad lives. His servants come to Ahab to plead for mercy, and receive a warm response (v 31-33).

> ❷ *What does Ahab gain from freeing Ben-Hadad in verse 34?*

⌃ Pray

God's grace to Ahab continues. He still speaks by his prophets, and when Ahab responds, God grants victory. Give thanks to God for his wonderful grace.

A missed opportunity

Read 1 Kings 20:35-43

> ❷ *What do the events of verses 35 and 37 underline about responding to the prophetic word?*

Having been struck, the prophet now looks like a wounded soldier.

> ❷ *Why does the prophet approach Ahab with a story in verses 38-40?*
> ❷ *What should Ahab have done, and why (v 41-2)?*

⌄ Apply

In sparing Ben-Hadad, Ahab has acted in his own interest, but not in God's. Unlike David, his heart was not devoted to the Lord, and he will be judged as a result.

> ❷ *1 Kings keeps challenging us to put the things of God first—even and perhaps especially when another way seems to be more "sensible". How do you need to respond to that challenge this day?*

❤ *Bible in a year: 1 Kings 10-11 • Matthew 8 v 18-34*

God, Ahab and Naboth

Ahab shows what kind of king he wants to be, but also reveals another side to his character.

Jezebel and Naboth
Read 1 Kings 21:1-16

❓ *What puts Ahab into a monumental sulk in verses 1-4?*

Naboth's refusal in verse 3 is based on passages such as Leviticus 25:23-28, which tell the Israelites they must not sell land permanently. Naboth's faithfulness highlights Ahab's flaws.

❓ *What does Jezebel's question in 1 Kings 21:7 reveal about her view of kingship?*

Jezebel acts in Ahab's name, and hatches a plot to have Naboth killed.

❓ *What does the response of the elders in verses 11-14 tell us about Israel at the time of Ahab and Jezebel?*

✅ Apply

Naboth the faithful Israelite is stoned to death, and Ahab gets his vineyard. Everything goes according to plan, and the elders of Jezreel who have gone along with all this can hardly object now. It looks like the perfect crime. Wickedness appears to have won. We need to recognise the reality of evil in Elijah's days, and in ours. This is how our lost world behaves, and it should grieve us, but not surprise us.

Elijah and Ahab
Read 1 Kings 21:17-29

It may look like the perfect crime, but God sees everything. He sends Elijah to confront Ahab, and then to pronounce judgment on the king and his family.

❓ *How does the judgment that Ahab will face fit the crime?*

❓ *Look at verses 25-26. Why else does Ahab face judgment?*

Ahab and his descendants face the same judgment as Jeroboam and Baasha (v 22). Ahab is the worst of them (v 25-26). Not only has he introduced idolatry into Israel's worship of God but he has led Israel after false gods, the Baal and Asherah. This makes what happens next a bit of a surprise.

❓ *How do you respond to verse 27?*

❓ *What changes as a result (v 28-29)?*

After the murder of Naboth, we rejoice that Ahab and Jezebel will receive what they deserve. But Ahab repents, and judgment is delayed. God is merciful to repentant sinners.

🔼 Pray

Pray for a heart that delights in the repentance of evildoers as God rejoices in the repentance of Ahab.

True and false prophecy

Micaiah the prophet reveals more of God's plan for Ahab.

Read 1 Kings 22:1-28

This chapter picks up on the events of chapter 20, and Ahab's wars with Aram. Ben-Hadad agreed to return captured cities to Israel in 20:34, but Aram still occupies Ramoth Gilead.

> ❷ *What does Jehoshaphat's response to Ahab in 22:4-5 reveal about his character?*

We met 450 prophets of Baal in 1 Kings 18. Here we meet 400 "prophets", who claim to speak for God. They offer an encouraging word, but Jehoshaphat isn't convinced.

There is another prophet who Ahab is reluctant to call. He is to be brought, and in verse 10 we see that he will come into an intimidating situation, facing a hostile king and 400 dodgy prophets.

> ❷ *What makes Zedekiah's message in verses 11-12 so attractive?*
> ❷ *What kind of prophet is Micaiah (v 13-14)?*

Micaiah prophesies, and initially appears to agree with the other prophets (v 15). However, even Ahab can tell that this is not the real message he brings (v 16).

> ❷ *Why does Ahab respond negatively to Micaiah's prophecy (v 17-18)?*
> ❷ *Micaiah gives us a glimpse of the heavenly throne room in verses 19-23. Why does God send a deceiving spirit into the mouths of the prophets?*

Even though the prophets are leading Ahab astray *by God's will*, the Lord still warns Ahab through Micaiah, and so gives him the opportunity to repent.

> ❷ *Zedekiah and Ahab both cast doubt on Micaiah's words in verses 24-28. Why does Micaiah respond in the way he does?*

⌄ Apply

We have seen some strange things happening with prophecy in 1 Kings so far, with the man of God in 1 Kings 13, and the prophet who came to Ahab in 1 Kings 20:35-43. However, here we wrestle with the problem of true and false prophecy. We see God at work both through the *true* prophecy of Micaiah, and the *false* pronouncements of the other prophets. We see the importance of discerning truth from falsehood, and the confidence we can have in true prophecy.

> ❷ *How do you know if a prophet speaks truthfully (v 28 is a hint)?*
> ❷ *What other tests might we apply to claims that someone is speaking direct from God?*
> ❷ *How does this give you confidence to trust the prophecies we read in God's word?*

⏷ *Bible in a year: 1 Kings 14-15 • Matthew 9 v 18-38*

The death of Ahab

Ahab takes elaborate precautions as he enters battle, but cannot avoid death, or the judgment God promised.

Read 1 Kings 22:29-40

Ahab won't listen to the warnings of Micaiah, but he does take precautions and disguises himself. He is less concerned about Jehoshaphat's safety!

- ❓ *Why is the king of Aram so focused on Ahab in verses 31-33?*
- ❓ *Ahab dies from a "random" arrow (v 34-35). What does this tell you about how God achieves his purposes?*

Ahab's death has a certain heroism, as he is propped in his chariot to preserve the morale of his troops. But as the sun sets on his life and the battle, their courage fails.

- ❓ *Why does the narrator emphasise the gory details about how Ahab died, and how the chariot was cleaned (v 35-38)?*

···· TIME OUT ·························

If you want to remind yourself of the various prophetic words that Ahab had received about what was going to happen to him and his family, have a look at **1 Kings 20:42; 21:19, 29.**

⌄ Apply

Of course the events here are far from random. 1 Kings shows us that God is sovereign over all these events, even over those who seek to do evil. Even in some of the darkest times in Israel's history, God still achieves his purposes

- ❓ *How does God's sovereignty impact how you think about your current situation?*

We then come to the final summary of Ahab's reign, including his other achievements in 22:39-40, as his son Ahaziah becomes king.

- ❓ *How does the information here impact how we think about Ahab?*
- ❓ *Why do you think these achievements only get a brief mention in 1 Kings?*

⌄ Apply

Ahab is a complicated character. He sulks, but he also repents. He is willing to listen to the prophetic word, for example in 1 Kings 18, but he doesn't always respond appropriately, and he is more obedient to Jezebel than he is to God. To many in the surrounding nations, he would have looked like a powerful king who won battles, built palaces and cities, and defended his people. Yet the evaluation of 1 Kings is very different. We need to be careful that our evaluation of both ourselves and others matches up with God's view.

⌃ Pray

Think about people you admire, support or revere for their achievements. Now pray for them according to the more important things: their spiritual life and influence on others.

Jehoshaphat and Ahaziah

After Ahab's death, we meet the next king of Israel, and the current king of Judah. 1 Kings closes with a tragic but hopeful summary of God's people and their kings.

Jehoshaphat

Read 1 Kings 22:41-50

We may almost have forgotten that Judah existed, given the concentration on the northern kingdom in the last seven chapters. Jehoshaphat came to power in Judah while Ahab was on the throne.

> ❓ *What kind of king was Jehoshaphat according to verses 43 and 44?*
> ❓ *What is, and what isn't, the author of Kings interested in (v 45-46)?*
> ❓ *What do you make of Jehoshaphat's attempt to make ships to go to Ophir for gold in verses 48 and 49? (You may wish to compare this account with 1 Kings 9:26-28.)*

Jehoshaphat's reign is briefly described, and we won't come to Jehoram his son until 2 Kings 8, as the focus on the northern kingdom continues. However, overall Jehoshaphat is portrayed in a positive light.

⌄ Apply

As we have seen before, all the kings we meet here are flawed and imperfect. Even the "good" kings point us to the need for a perfect king, which keeps us looking forward to the coming of Jesus Christ, the perfect son of David.

Ahaziah

Read 1 Kings 22:51-53

Ahaziah gets a very brief mention, although his reign is also dealt with in 2 Kings 1. It is worth remembering that the division between the two books is only because of the length of the scrolls on which they were written, so the two books belong together.

> ❓ *How is Ahaziah evaluated?*
> ❓ *Given what we have already seen in 1 Kings, what will happen to Ahaziah?*
> ❓ *Compare the evaluations in this passage of Jehoshaphat and Ahaziah. What is it that makes a good king a good king?*

⌄ Apply

Sometimes the kings come and go very quickly, sometimes we spend a lot of time with a particular ruler, as we have with Ahab and Solomon. The kings are inconsistent, but God's word remains constant, and he keeps his promises, blessing his faithful people and judging those who rebel against him and turn to idols. 1 Kings teaches us that we can rely on God's word, even when people let us down.

> ❓ *These words are written for our encouragement, warning and instruction. How would you sum up what you have learned from 1 Kings?*

Try to talk to a friend—Christian or not—about your thoughts today.

The measure of our days

The context of this tricky little psalm is a little difficult to fathom. It seems that David is desperate not to speak his mind in front of pagans.

Whatever the precise circumstances, death is foremost in his mind...

Read Psalm 39:1-3

❓ *What has David decided to do (v 1)?*
❓ *Why do you think he feels the need to keep silent in front of the pagans (v 1b)?*

Presumably he felt that they will not understand, or will mock him and his trust in God (see v 8). Perhaps he is the object of derision, because God has disciplined him for sin (v 11) by humbling him publicly and taking away his wealth. Eventually he bursts out at them (v 3)—and his shame at his failure and their misunderstanding brings him to his knees.

✔ Apply

How do you represent failure and setbacks to non-believers (or even to fellow Christians)? "I'm having a hard time; I'm down on my luck; I'm going through the mill..." If we truly believed in a sovereign God of providence, should we not rather be saying things like: "God is teaching me patience; he's showing me not to trust in money; he's teaching me to remember I'm mortal..."?

This mortal coil

Read Psalm 39:4-6

❓ *Why is it so important that we know how fleeting our life is (v 6)?*

✔ Apply

David makes an application that is both despairing and comforting. Death makes life fundamentally meaningless for those with no God. But for believers, why do we get so worked up about things, and so stuck on acquiring wealth? From the perspective of eternity, the trivia that consume our minds daily is just so much wasted energy.

The real hope of life

Read Psalm 39:7-13

❓ *Thinking about death and an unknown future, what does David do (v 7)?*
❓ *And what does he know is the most important thing to be sure of (v 8a)?*

Verse 13 seems despairing: he wants God's rebuking gaze to move away from him, so that he can enjoy life before it's over. It's perhaps understandable from one who did not know much about the glories to come. But for us who live after the cross and resurrection, things are different...

✔ Pray

Spend some time thanking God for the sure hope of heaven, and for the knowledge that suffering and discipline are part of his good purposes to prepare us for glory.

If you have time, **read Revelation 21:1-8** and rejoice in your future.

"My deliverer"

When you face overwhelming circumstances, where do you turn first?

A God who saves

Read Psalm 40:1-5

❷ *What was David's situation?*
❷ *What happened to change it?*
❷ *Where does David exhort us to turn?*
❷ *Why not turn to the proud?*
❷ *How might we "go astray after a lie" (v 4)?*
❷ *How does David react to what God has done for him?*

A God of grace

Read Psalm 40:6-11

❷ *What is David excited about? So what does he do?*
❷ *How do you want to respond to all that God has done for you?*

David is the Lord's anointed king ("Messiah"), but also a human being in need of salvation. He too needs God's mercy, love and faithfulness to preserve him. Verse 6 reminds us that only God can cure our spiritual deafness and enable us to hear his word where it matters: in our hearts.

🔼 Pray

Rejoice that you have heard God speak to you and that he enabled you to turn to him in repentance and faith.

Ask him to give you the desire to do his will, and to imprint his law on your heart.

🔽 Apply

We all sometimes feel we've let God down. It's easy to feel he either can't or won't use us again.

❷ *What encouragement does verse 11 give you, to carry with you into times like that?*

It's important, while times are good, to see what God has done for us and rejoice—so that when things turn bad, we don't let go of God and lose sight of the comfort he wants to give us.

A God who protects

Read Psalm 40:12-17

❷ *Where does David see that his troubles have come from?*

His enemies want to emphasise his failings and failures. We see it all the time in politics: someone's always absolutely sure they would have done things better.

❷ *What's your response when someone else fails in a responsibility?*
❷ *"Poor and needy" is a term David often uses for himself. What do you think it means? How can we follow David's example?*

🔽 Apply

❷ *Will God ever leave you in the lurch?*
❷ *How does this psalm help you to realise that's never going to happen?*

 Bible in a year: 2 Kings 1-3 • Matthew 12 v 1-23

LUKE: When all seems lost

When we are at the end of our resources, when all our hope is gone, when decay and death are right before us—Jesus is there.

The centurion
Read Luke 7:1-10

A soldier's highly-valued servant is on the point of death (v 2).

> ❷ *Why do the Jewish elders think the centurion deserves Jesus' help (v 4-5)?*
> ❷ *What does the centurion himself believe he deserves from Jesus (v 6)?*

He knows Jesus has the *authority* to help (v 7-8) but he knows he has no right to Jesus' help. So the question is: does Jesus have the *willingness* to help?

> ❷ *What does Jesus do for the servant (v 10)?*
> ❷ *What does Jesus commend about the centurion (v 9)?*

···· **TIME OUT** ····························

Read James 4:6-10

Here's a wonderful paradox at the heart of the Christian faith. Those who feel themselves deserving, receive nothing from God: those who know they are totally undeserving, are given everything by God. We see this repeatedly in Luke. The self-proclaimed deserving get nothing from Jesus; the self-admitted undeserving are given time, friendship, healing, life.

> ❷ *How does this encourage and challenge you today?*

The widow
Read Luke 7:11-17

This woman's dearly-loved son has died. She's buried her husband; now she's burying her only child.

> ❷ *Has there been an experience in your life similar to this? Can you imagine how this lady is feeling?*
> ❷ *How does the Lord Jesus feel about her situation (v 13)?*

But Jesus doesn't only *feel* for this woman...

> ❷ *What might you have thought and felt if you had been there?*

Where Jesus is, there is a future beyond death. In Jesus, there can be family beyond death. If you have a loved one who died trusting Jesus, one day they will be given back to you by the Lord.

Look forward to that day, and praise God!

▲ Pray

What a wonderful phrase verse 13 is! We have a Lord who, though the stars and planets were made by him, still has a heart which goes out to each one of us when we struggle and grieve.

Thank the Lord Jesus for who he is. Thank him that he is there for you when you face pain and bereavement.

Are you the one?

Do you ever doubt who Jesus really is? If you do, you've got something in common with the greatest man who ever lived (before Jesus came along)…

You, or someone else?

TIME OUT

Read Isaiah 35:3-7; 61:1

- ❓ *Who is coming (35:4)?*
- ❓ *How can his coming be recognised (v 5-7; 61:1)?*

Read Luke 7:18-23

John the Baptist is in prison (Luke 3:19-20). And as he sits there, his public Jesus-pointing ministry over, he begins to worry…

- ❓ *What's his concern (Luke 7:19-20)?*

Think back to what you've just seen God promising through Isaiah.

- ❓ *Why is Jesus' response in verse 22 so powerful?*

You matter

Read Luke 7:24-28

Jesus reminds the people that they didn't go into the desert on a safari trip, or for a fashion parade—they went to hear what John, God's messenger said (v 24-26).

- ❓ *What was the point of John's ministry (v 27)?*

If Jesus wasn't the way God came to his world, John's ministry and suffering were worthless. But because Jesus is "the one who [is] to come" (v 19), "there is no one greater than John" (v 28); no Old Testament God-given job was more important than his.

- ❓ *But how does John compare to any member of God's kingdom (v 28)?*

Telling people that Jesus is God's King isn't easy, and often brings rejection. Is it worth it? Jesus says: "Yes!" *Why?* Because Jesus is exactly who he said he was.

☑ Apply

- ❓ *Have you appreciated the privilege of being part of the kingdom of God?*
- ❓ *And have you grasped the eternal value of announcing to others that Jesus is the King of that kingdom?*

You can't win

Read Luke 7:29-35

- ❓ *Why did the Pharisees ignore John (v 33)?*
- ❓ *Why did they criticise Jesus (v 34)?*

John was honestly wondering about Jesus—he got a clear answer. The Pharisees were determined to find fault—they missed the answer.

- ❓ *If John were around in your church, would you look down on him as taking it all a bit too seriously?*
- ❓ *If Jesus were part of your church, would you look down on him because of the people he hung around with?*

 Bible in a year: 2 Kings 7-9 • Matthew 13 v 1-30

She loved much

Ever heard the one about the King, the pastor and the prostitute? It's seriously shocking.

Shocking entrance
Read Luke 7:36-39

Jesus is at a dinner party in a house at the respectable end of town. As was common, they're lying down round the table (v 36).

> ❷ Why would the events of verses 37-38 cause a stir?
> ❷ What do we find out about this woman (v 37, 39)?
> ❷ Why is she "weeping" (v 38), do you think?

Probably, she is a prostitute. Certainly, she is someone who has lived publicly in a way which rejects God. Everyone knows "what kind of woman she is".

> ❷ Why is the reaction of Simon the Pharisee' in verse 39 so understandable?

Shocking response
Read Luke 7:40-50

> ❷ What is Christ's reaction (v 48, 50)?
> ❷ How does Jesus compare the religious leader and the woman (v 44-45)?
> ❷ How does his parable (v 41-43) explain why the lady and the Pharisee treat Jesus so differently?

Imagine that two visitors turned up at your church on Sunday: a pastor and a prostitute.

> ❷ Who would find the bigger welcome?
> ❷ Who would you make the effort to go and say "hello" to first?

See **James 2:1-5** for another example of this situation.

Real love

If we consider ourselves deserving of having Jesus in our lives, we'll act towards him like the Pharisee did. He did what those around him would have expected—but no more. He treated Jesus with respect—but he did not love him.

If we realise we're like the woman—owing God an infinite debt, and piling up more and more debt each day—we'll treat Jesus like she did. She didn't care what others thought of her. There was nothing she would not do for him. She loved him.

If we've grasped Christ's forgiveness, it will melt our hearts. Every part of our lives will be offered to him—none of it off-limits. There'll be no part of our life we don't want to serve him with. We'll weep with grief at our sin, and we'll weep with joy at our forgiveness. We'll love him.

⌃ Pray

Approach Jesus now as the woman did.

Admit to him ways in which you've sinned recently; acknowledge you deserve nothing from him; thank him with all your heart for his forgiveness; and offer all that you have and are to him.

Ears to hear?

Sometimes, things can go in one ear, and out the other. But when that happens with Jesus' words to us, it should be a matter of serious concern…

A parable about soil

Read Luke 8:1-8, 11-15

Verses 4-8 are the parable; and verses 11-15 are the Lord's handy explanation of his meaning. It's a story which explains how God's word, the "seed" (v 11), will be received.

> ❷ *Use the two passages to fill in the table (the third column isn't from the passage):*

Soil	Reaction to God's word	How this looks in reality today
path	heard – forgotten	Vague idea of God but reject it, will fall away
rock	readily joyful gave up	make a commitment at an event but no progress
thorn	heard, pride to dwell on earthly concerns	falling away
good	hearty, growth, produce fruit	growing, mature, God's will, does God's will

Why a parable at all?

Why does Jesus use parables? Why not just talk plainly?!

Read Luke 8:9-10

The disciples don't understand the parable (v 9); but they bother to ask for an explanation.

> ❷ *Why does Jesus speak to the crowds in parables (v 10)?*

> ❷ *How are the disciples different to the crowds (v 10)?*
> ❷ *Why?*

Do we have the humility to ask Jesus to teach us (v 9)? Do we have ears that are willing to listen (v 8), and hearts willing to be changed by Jesus (v 15)? If we do, he'll give us the "secrets of the kingdom of God"—who its King is, how we can enter it, and how we can live as part of it.

On the other hand, how easy is it for Jesus' words—at church, in a small group, in Bible-reading notes—to go in one ear and out the other, without getting anywhere near our hearts!

⌄ Apply

It doesn't take long to realise that Jesus is right. Tragically, some people turn out to be rocky or thorny soil.

> ❷ *How does Jesus' parable help us when this happens?*

Flick through the last few *Explore* studies, or think back to Sunday's sermon.

> ❷ *Did you retain and live out what you heard?*

Would it help to memorise a verse each time? Or set an alarm to remind you to think about it? Or make a note and stick it up? Or tell someone what your application is?

Light, house, family

When someone switches on a light, they do it for a very good reason: so that people can see what is there. Light, quite simply, illuminates.

Revealing light

Read Luke 8:16-18

In this parable the "lamp" stands for Jesus' words, just as the "seed" did in his previous one (v 11). And Jesus will never stop holding out his word (v 16).

- ❓ *Why is this challenging (v 17)?*
- ❓ *Why is it important that when we listen, we're willing to be changed (v 18)?*

The religious leaders "think they have" many things. They assume they are already in God's kingdom. They keep lots of religious rules; they are regulars at the synagogue. But their response to the light of Christ's teaching is disclosing the reality that they don't really know God. Jesus is warning them: one day, you'll lose even what you do have.

- ❓ *What would be the equivalent today?*

⌄ Apply

Listening to Jesus is unsettling. It exposes what we're really like. The easy option is to seek to block it out—but that leads to disaster (v 18). The harder, but infinitely better, choice is to let Jesus shine his light into every part of life, so we can deal with ways we're not living for him.

- ❓ *What areas of your life would you rather keep in the dark, "hidden" from Jesus' searching words?*

Family values

Read Luke 8:19-21

Jesus is, it seems, in a large house. But it's full of people, and so his relatives can't get near him. And he takes this opportunity to encourage those who have made the hard choice to listen to and live out his teaching.

- ❓ *What does Jesus say about people who do live out what he says?*
- ❓ *Remember who Jesus is, and who his Father is. Why is verse 21 exciting for every Christian?*

It's one of the most wonderful truths of Scripture: that if we are a follower of Christ, we are a brother or sister of Christ, and a child of the Father. Everything that is Jesus' is ours. His death was ours; his eternal life is ours; his glory and inheritance will be ours. How wonderful to know that the eternal Son of God says to us: *You're family.*

⌃ Pray

Thank your brother Jesus for bringing you into the Father's family. Pray that you would bring honour to the family in how you put God's word into practice today.

Lord of the storms

It's one thing to be able to forecast the weather. It's quite another to be able to make it.

Read Luke 8:22-25

Master and Commander

- ❓ *What's the situation by the end of v 23?*
- ❓ *How do the disciples—some of whom are experienced fishermen—react (v 24)?*
- ❓ *What does Jesus do (v 24)?*

TIME OUT

Read Psalm 104:1-7. There's only one person who can control the waters with a rebuke (v 7): the Lord God himself.

- ❓ *What is the right response to him (v 1)?*
- ❓ *Why is the disciples' question in Luke 8:25 the right one to be asking?*
- ❓ *What's the answer they should be coming to?*

Disciples, then and now

In a way, there are two "rebukes" here. One is to the chaos of the storm, calming it (v 24). The other is to the disciples' faithless fear (v 25). The disciples understood half of what they needed to know. They knew that the storm was so great that "we're going to drown". They recognised their utter helplessness when faced with a world that goes wrong.

But they had not yet learned to have faith in the one who controls creation. They had not yet understood that however great the storm, they were with one who was still more powerful.

- ❓ *Imagine that Jesus hadn't gone to sleep, or had not allowed the storm even to start. What wouldn't his followers have learned about:*
  - *who he is?*
  - *what faith is?*

✔ Apply

- ❓ *In your life, when things are going wrong, and when Jesus seems absent, what do you do? Do you look at the storm and panic, or do you look to your Lord and trust?*
- ❓ *Where in your life do you need to apply the truths of this passage?*

⌃ Pray

- ❓ *Are you enduring a storm at the moment? Or can you see one brewing on the horizon?*

Speak to Jesus now. Thank him that he is the God who is in control. Thank him that he is the God who is in your life. Thank him that he will bring you through.

And then (this is the hard bit!) ask him to use the storm to help you know him better, and not to still it until you have learned to trust him more.

 Bible in a year: 2 Kings 17-18 • Matthew 15 v 1-20

Blessing in trouble

We're not in David's shoes (thank God), but he shows us where to place our confidence and trust when things look bad.

"I'm really feeling blessed."

You've maybe heard someone say that when times are good. But what if things go awry?

Read Psalm 41:1-3

> ❷ *Does God keep those who love and obey him out of all trouble?*
> ❷ *What does God do for those he loves?*

"Everyone hates me"

Read Psalm 41:4-10

> ❷ *What is similar about verses 4 and 10?*

This psalm is typical of Hebrew poetry. It's like a sandwich: the lines and verses are like layers of bread, spread and fillings, that mirror each other until we reach the meat at the core.

> ❷ *Can you see how verses 5 and 9, 6 and 8 mirror each other's ideas, and verse 7 is the core?*

David's sandwich has a bitter filling.

> ❷ *What do David's enemies wish for him?*
> ❷ *Have you ever been in a situation where others have actively wished you ill?*
> ❷ *How would you want to respond in such a situation?*

Pray that you would have a similar godly attitude when you are faced with similar circumstances.

"You have upheld me"

Read Psalm 41:11-12

These verses correspond with verses 1-3.

> ❷ *What is the "bread and butter" that holds David's sandwich together?*

David trusts absolutely in God. He knows that God uses all circumstances to form him into the man he wants David to be; even illness, palace intrigues and plots, and active, malicious ill-will that David hears of all around him in his time of weakness.

His integrity is not sinlessness (he knows all too well his own failings), but his confidence in the God who has made a covenant with his people, and a covenant with David himself. God will never let him go, will never abandon him to the malevolence of his enemies.

Coda

Read Psalm 41:13

The Psalms are divided into 5 "books". This verse acts as an "end sheet" for Book 1, Psalms 1 – 41. David has learned and shared so much about God as he has composed these psalms.

> ❷ *What is his response?*
> ❷ *Who does he want to bless?*
> ❷ *How do you respond to God in the light of what the psalms tell you about him?*

Bible in a year: 2 Kings 19-21 • Matthew 15 v 21-39

Who's afraid?

Fear now becomes a recurring theme. Can there be anything more terrifying than being confronted with someone who is out of control, and in the grip of evil? Actually, yes, there can…

Jesus and the demons
Read Luke 8:26-33

We're diving into Luke straight after Jesus has calmed a storm (v 23-24). But if his disciples thought that was the end of their terror for that day, they were wrong.

❓ *Who confronts Jesus on the shore (v 27)?*

Use the details of verse 27 and the end of verse 29 to picture the scene. *Terrifying!*

❓ *Yet who is afraid (v 28)? Why (v 29)?*

It's an unexpected role reversal. "Many demons had gone into" this man (v 30). Yet Jesus is calm and in control—and the demons are powerless and begging.

❓ *What happens to the demons (v 32-33)?*
❓ *What does demonic possession do to creatures (including humans)?*
❓ *What does this episode tell us about Jesus?*

···· TIME OUT ·················

Some cultures dismiss the idea of demons—but then lack an explanation for where evil comes from. Others know there are evil spirits—and live in fear.

❓ *How is what we see of Jesus here good news, and challenging news, for both cultures?*

Imagine you live nearby, and you hear what Jesus has done for this man.

❓ *How would you react, do you think?*

Read Luke 8:34-39

❓ *What is surprising about the reaction of the locals (v 34-37)?*
❓ *What are they afraid of (v 35, 37)?*

We're not told exactly why they felt this. But whatever the reason, they see the Lord Jesus at work—and ask him to leave. They're more afraid of the presence of the Lord than they are of the presence of evil.

❓ *How does Jesus respond (v 37)?*
❓ *What is the right way to react to the Lord (v 38-39)?*

✔ Apply

Jesus has authority over everything. And yet how often we would rather he left us alone to our comfortable lives, rather than asking us to do hard things and take risks and trust him.

Are you not asking or allowing Jesus to be Lord in some area of your life, because you're afraid of the consequences?

Will you trust the all-powerful Jesus with that area right now, leaving the outcome of living his way up to him?

Hope in everything

Jesus is attaining celebrity status. As he returns from his Gerasene excursion, a crowd is waiting for him. And among that crowd are two desperate people.

A dying girl
Read Luke 8:40-42

> ❓ *How is Jairus described (v 41)?*
> ❓ *Why might it be surprising that this man is willing to fall at Jesus' feet?*

How worthless our reputation seems when a loved one needs help!

> ❓ *What does it seem that Jesus will do (see the end of v 42)?*

A sick woman
Read Luke 8:43-49

> ❓ *How is the woman described (v 43)?*

This would have left her constantly unclean, according to Jewish law (see Leviticus 15:25-31). She has been an outcast from God's people for twelve long years—until today.

> ❓ *What does she do (Luke 8:44)? What happens?*

To come to Jesus in trust is to be restored to kingdom cleanliness. The woman is healed—and we'd expect that to be the end of the story. But Jesus stops, asks who touched him, and refuses to let the matter drop (v 45-46).

> ❓ *What does the woman end up having to do (v 47)?*
> ❓ *What does Jesus explain to her (v 48)?*

TIME OUT

> ❓ *Why does Jesus act like this?*

The woman needs to know that it is not reaching out her hand that caused her to be healed; it was the faith that caused her to reach out her hand. And she needs to see that faith in Jesus is not to be kept secret; his work in her life is to be shared with others.

We need to remember both of these things too.

A dead girl
Read Luke 8:49-56

> ❓ *What has now happened (v 49)?*
> ❓ *How does Jesus respond (v 50)?*
> ❓ *What does he then do (v 54)?*

Jesus lets both the woman and Jairus reach a place where all earthly hope is gone. For those who do not know Jesus, beyond human hope lies only fear (v 50). With Jesus, beyond it lies faith—real hope—in the one who can restore us, no matter how long or how deep our struggles.

✔ Apply

> ❓ *Can you think of a time in your life when all other hope had gone? How did you learn to truly trust in Christ in that period?*
> ❓ *Where does "just believing" need to make a difference in your life today?*

Bible in a year: 2 Kings 24-25 • Matthew 17

Working for the kingdom

So far, Jesus has done all his kingdom-announcing, kingdom-showing work himself. Now, he begins to delegate.

Privilege
Read Luke 9:1-4

❷ *What does Jesus enable the Twelve to do (v 1-2)?*
❷ *Who has been doing these things before?*
❷ *Why is the disciples' new role a great privilege?*

This is not a lucrative job! Kingdom-preachers, like their master, are not to be wealthy in worldly terms. They are not to be self-reliant (v 3). They are not to seek to climb the social ladder if their teaching proves popular (v 4).

This is, though, an immensely privileged job. Jesus is showing that his normal way of building his kingdom is by working through his people—all his people (see Matthew 28:18-20). He gives us the authority and ability to do what he did on earth—to make his name known, to preach his kingdom, to show his power.

Rejection
Read Luke 9:5-6

❷ *What does Jesus warn will sometimes happen (v 5)?*
❷ *Why does he tell his followers this, do you think?*

✓ Apply

"So they set out" (v 6). Jesus had "called his

disciples to him" (Luke 6:13), and now he had sent them out from him.

If you are a Christian, the Lord has called you to spend time with him, to know him, to learn from him. What a privilege! And he has called you to set out among the people around you, to preach him, to show him. What a privilege!

❷ *How are you doing these things in your life? Could you be doing more of them?*

Report
Read Luke 9:7-10

The powerful political elite, such as King Herod, are beginning to ask questions (v 9). The ordinary people will sometimes "not welcome you" (v 5). But neither unwelcome attention nor outright rejection are to sway Jesus' people from doing Jesus' work. Ultimately, there is only one person they need to report to: the Lord himself (v 10).

✦ Pray

Read Luke 19:11-15. All Jesus' followers will one day give a report to our King for how we have used the gifts, roles and opportunities he has given us.

Thank him now for making you part of his work in his world. Ask him now to help you to do the work he has given you to do.

The Master's banquet

This is one of the most famous episodes in the Gospels. But perhaps it will have a few surprises for us.

Read Luke 9:10-17

The Master

❓ *Where is the action taking place (v 12)?*

The problem is that there simply isn't enough food (v 13-14).

❓ *What does Jesus do (v 16)?*
❓ *What's the result (v 17)?*

Read Exodus 16:1-18

❓ *Where is the action taking place (v 2-3)?*

The problem is... there simply isn't enough food (v 3)!

❓ *What does God do (v 4, 14-15)?*
❓ *What's the result (v 18)?*
❓ *What is Jesus teaching his people through this event, do you think?*

Providing miraculous food in the wilderness is a God-like thing to do. And while Moses could only point people to the God who provides, in the remote place near Bethsaida, Jesus points to himself as the God who provides.

This feeding of the 5,000 is, first and foremost, a lesson about who Jesus is. In verses Luke 9:7-9, Herod had wondered if he was a prophet (like Moses). The loaves and fishes prove he is much, much more than that.

The followers

❓ *Who does Jesus say should feed these people (v 13)?*
❓ *Who does actually physically feed the people (end of v 16)?*

Again we see Jesus working through his people. And here, we see his servants learning to look to him to give them the resources to feed the hungry. Verse 13 forces them to recognise their own limitations—verse 16 points them to the one who knows no limitations.

❓ *How does everyone end up feeling (v 17)?*

▾ Apply

Do you look to Jesus to satisfy you? Where else are you tempted to look for what you need in life?

When you minister to people—from a pulpit, in a small group, over a coffee, or in another way—do you ask the Lord to provide you with what you need to care for them? And do you make sure you are pointing them to Jesus as the one who satisfies?

▴ Pray

Lord Jesus, help me today and every day to turn to you to find what truly satisfies. And help me to offer to others the satisfaction of life with you. *Amen.*

The suffering King

These words may be familiar to some of us. But they must never be less than deeply challenging…

King

Read Luke 9:18-20

Jesus asks for an opinion poll about who he is. And all the answers fall within the category of "prophet": God's messenger.

❓ *How does Peter's view differ (v 20)?*

Peter has grasped something crucial. Jesus is not a prophet, pointing to the coming of God's all-powerful King, the Christ; he is the one the prophets predicted. Jesus isn't a messenger; he's the message.

The question "Who is Jesus?" is one we must all answer. Jesus is not interested in our background, what our relatives think, what our church says. His priority is our hearts. Our opinion. Our readiness to recognise him as the Christ of God.

Many people today give Jesus what looks like a position of respect—wise teacher, moral philosopher, important prophet. But if we don't bow to him as the Christ, then we're insulting him. It's like meeting the queen of Great Britain and treating her as the mayor of a town.

Killed

Read Luke 9:21-25

❓ *What does Jesus say will be done to him as God's all-powerful King (v 22)?*

Imagine you are a disciple. You've seen him calm storms, reverse death, evict demons.

❓ *Why would his words here shock you?*
❓ *How are Jesus' words to his followers a challenge, today as then (v 23-25)?*
❓ *What is the answer to Jesus' question in verse 25? Why is it easy to forget this?*

This wasn't the Christ Israel was expecting—or the Christ his disciples thought they were following. They expected pomp and popularity to be the path to glory; not suffering and service as Jesus says.

☑ Apply

What do you think life as a Christian will be like between now and your death? Easy? Comfortable? How do you need the reality check of Jesus' words here?

Glory

Read Luke 9:26-27

❓ *What will happen in the future (v 26)?*

Jesus will rule in unimaginable glory. The road there leads uphill, for his followers as for him—but the other path, of disowning him for comfort's sake now, will lead to him disowning us then (v 26).

⌃ Pray

Pray that you would never forget the identity and future of Jesus. Ask God to help you take up your cross, to serve and to suffer on your way to glory.

Longing for God

At times, talk of "the joy of the Lord," and of "celebrating his love" seems hollow and mocking. This unnamed psalmist has encouraged believers down the ages to keep going when spiritual life seems to have drained out of them.

Read Psalms 42 and 43

Commentators agree that these two psalms belong together. So that's how we'll read them in the next couple of weeks.

The absent God

Read Psalm 42:1-2

You've been there: a hot, dry day—you needed a drink but couldn't get one. Thirst is a consuming need for refreshment that just can't be ignored.

Sometimes spiritual life is like that. God feels far away; we think we can never get back to our former experience of relationship with him. Even church, once so enthusing, seems a drag.

> ❷ *Do you know how that feels (now, or previously)?*

You're not alone. God put this psalm in Scripture because it's a common experience. He knows that sometimes we can feel he's gone AWOL. But he hasn't.

···· **TIME OUT** ························

God knows how it feels. Jesus experienced it on the cross.

Read Mark 15:33-37; John 19:28-30

The unseen God

Read Psalm 42:3

Israel had a God, but no idols (officially). So those who ignored the first and second commandments taunted those who kept them, and the surrounding nations did too (Psalm 79:10; 115:2). If you couldn't see an idol, how could you know what your god was like? Of course God can never be depicted adequately by an image. Yet he is ever-present, seen in his actions, heard in his word.

> ❷ *How have you seen God at work in your own experience?*
> ❷ *If someone said to you, "Where is your God?", what would you point them to?*

The faithful God

Read Psalm 42:4-5

Our psalmist uses memories of joyful occasions to remind himself of God's reliability, in spite of his volatile emotions. He says to himself, *Why are you cast down?*, and reminds himself of God's faithfulness to his people. Despite spiritual dryness and depression, he determines that the facts he knows will override the feelings he experiences.

Never forget, God never lets his children go.

Pray

Pray for anyone you know who's spiritually drained, depressed, feeling far from God. If that's you, use this psalm to encourage yourself.

Far-away God

It's ok to feel lost, alone, abandoned. And it's ok to express that to God.

Read Psalms 42 and 43

It's helpful to remember the larger whole as we're reading today's passage.

The downcast believer

Read Psalm 42:6-7

Jordan, Hermon and Mizar were landmarks in Israel: the lowest point in the land, and the highest. Wherever he is, however he feels, our psalmist can always call God to mind.

Water and the sea are OT images often used to represent the world's rebellion against God. Our psalmist lives, like us, in tumultuous times. But he refuses to deny either how he feels, or what he knows about God.

Spiritual depression may accompany clinical depression (or not); it is real, and there's no shame in it. We too may feel overwhelmed by events and circumstances, and our emotional reaction to them. Our psalmist encourages us to say, "I won't let this dominate my life". Instead he purposefully remembers what God has done for his people.

❷ *What could you do when events and circumstances threaten to overwhelm you?*

The steadfast believer

Read Psalm 42:8-9

If we let go of God, times of depression are unbearably desolate (v 3). But if we hold on

to God then we can hope, even as we weep.

God's steadfast love is a key Old Testament idea. It's the love God promises in his covenants to those who remain faithful to him—even when they prove humanly weak and full of failure.

❷ *Will you determine to keep coming back to God, no matter what happens?*

The Hebrew for "Why have you forgotten me?" is almost identical to Jesus' cry on the cross, "Why have you forsaken me?" Jesus felt forsaken—but check out Luke 23:46.

❷ *Can you hold on to the memory of God, even when he seems to have forgotten you?*

The wounded believer

Read Psalm 42:10-11

It's terribly wounding when people use our low points to torture us. But God knows all about it. He's been there, in Jesus. Our psalmist is determined not to let suffering stop him worshipping the God who saves him.

⌄ Apply

When you're at your lowest, will you still worship God, and receive his comfort? It doesn't necessarily take away the suffering, but it makes it more bearable.

Seeing the King

Jesus had promised some of his followers that they would "see the kingdom of God" before their deaths (v 27). They didn't have long to wait…

A glimpse
Read Luke 9:28-33

This scene takes place far from the hustle and bustle of the crowds. We're with Jesus and his three closest friends, up a mountain.

> ❷ *What happens (v 29-31)?*

This is a glimpse of King Jesus' glory; a glimpse of the heavenly court, where even Moses and Elijah, men so greatly used by God, are clearly mere "men" standing beside the one clothed in incomparable "glory" (v 32). We are on the edge of human powers of description and understanding here. It's unsurprising that Peter has no idea what he's saying (v 33)!

···· **TIME OUT** ··

"Departure" in verse 31 is literally "exodus".

Read Exodus 12:21-32

> ❷ *How were the Israelites rescued from God's judgment (v 23)?*

This exodus was a wonderful signpost to the greater exodus Jesus would "bring to fulfilment at Jerusalem" (9:31), as he died.

> ❷ *How does the exodus in Egypt help us understand and appreciate what Jesus did at Jerusalem?*

A challenge
Read Luke 9:34-36

The "cloud" (v 34) is a sign of the presence of God himself (see Exodus 13:21; 1 Kings 8:10-13).

> ❷ *What does God the Father say (Luke 9:35)?*
> ❷ *What does he add here to what he said at Jesus' baptism (3:22)?*

Remember what Christ has just told his followers about what will happen to him, and how they must live as his followers (9:22-24). The question is: will they listen to him? Will they accept that he is King, of earth and of heaven, and that he tells them how life will be, for himself and for them? Or will they try to tell him how he should be, and what their life as his subjects should be like?

Will they listen to him? Will we?

☑ Apply

> ❷ *In which areas of life do you find it hard to listen to Jesus?*
> ❷ *How does this glimpse of his heavenly glory encourage and challenge you to listen to him?*
> ❷ *How does this glimpse encourage you in your prayers?*

Back down to earth

After a glimpse of heaven, we are brought crashing down to the reality of this fallen world. The cloud of God's presence is replaced by a crowd of unbelieving humans.

Not believing

Read Luke 9:37-43a

> ❓ *What is the problem that confronts Jesus (v 38-39)?*
> ❓ *What had the disciples failed to do (v 40)?*

We're being brought face to face with the destructive desire of evil (v 39). Without Jesus—the suffering, glorious Christ— destruction is the destiny of all.

> ❓ *What is shocking about Jesus' response (v 41)?*
> ❓ *Look at who is being talked about in verse 40. Who must Jesus' criticism of verse 41 include?*

But now the man is begging not Jesus' followers, but the Lord himself (v 38).

> ❓ *How does Christ respond (v 42)?*

⌄ Apply

In Mark, we discover the reason the disciples could not help this boy: they had not prayed (Mark 9:28-29). They were relying on themselves, not Jesus.

When the church stops believing in the power of Jesus to solve the needs of the world, the world is lost indeed. When we look to ourselves, instead of looking to and listening to and pleading with Jesus, the church becomes no more than a social club, and no more useful.

⌃ Pray

Pray for your church now. Pray that you would always look to and listen to Jesus. Ask that he would never find you unbelieving.

Not listening

Read Luke 9:43b-45

> ❓ *What does Jesus again attempt to explain to his followers (v 44)?*

Jesus is urging his followers to do just what his Father had told them to do (v 35)—to listen to him. But they just don't get it. They understand the words, but not their significance. And it seems as if they don't want to—they are afraid to ask (v 45). Whereas once they asked Jesus to explain himself (8:9), now they would rather not.

⌄ Apply

Again, the challenge to us as Jesus' followers is whether we are willing to listen to him as our King, or whether we would rather redefine him, soften him, change him. The world is full of false "Jesus Christs". Only one is real. Only one can save. Only one can make the difference in a world gripped by evil.

When do you find Jesus' teaching hard to agree with, to love, to obey? That will be the place where you are most likely to ask Jesus to change, instead of letting him change you.

The don't-dos of discipleship

Status, power, relationships. Three things we naturally yearn for and chase after. And three things towards which, if we're members of Christ's kingdom, our attitude will change radically.

Status

Read Luke 9:46-48

❓ *What's the argument about (v 46)?*
❓ *Look at what Jesus says in verse 48. How is this a rebuke to the disciples?*

In Jewish society, children were only occasionally seen, and certainly not heard. They were not worth the attention of serious people. Yet in the kingdom, status is not measured by achievement, contacts, reputation—but by caring for the excluded, the ignored, the vulnerable.

Power

Read Luke 9:49-56

❓ *What mistake did John make (v 49-50)?*
❓ *How can this same mistake be made in churches today?*

Jesus has mentioned those who are "against you" (v 50).

❓ *What's the sign that someone truly is "against" Jesus and his kingdom (v 53)?*

If power is our motivator, then we will seek to have it, keep it—and to not share it. John and the disciples loved being Jesus' followers, with the power to drive out demons (9:1)—they didn't want to share it. But Christ's kingdom isn't about focusing on our power and influence, rejecting those who are not "one of us".

How easy it is to be suspicious of fellow Christians who are not "one of us" (whoever "us" is). We can be far too quick to reject those who follow Jesus, who work "in [his] name" (v 49), simply because they speak or minister differently to us.

Of course, not everyone who says "Lord, Lord" about Jesus is really his follower (see 6:46). Truth must be contended for; false followers opposed. But we must beware of drawing the boundaries too tightly because, deep down, we enjoy the power of saying who is "in" (us) and who is "out" (them).

Relationships

Read Luke 9:57-62

❓ *Why are Jesus' words here deeply challenging?*
❓ *What is the Lord teaching about our view of our families and our view of his kingdom?*

☑ Apply

❓ *Status. Power. Relationships. Which do you tend to prioritise?*
❓ *How might that be at the expense of "service in the kingdom" (v 62)?*
❓ *Think back to what we've seen in Luke's Gospel of God's kingdom and its King, Jesus. Why is this more important than anything else we might chase in life?*

The harvest field and you

When you think about mission, what do you think of? Christian work that happens abroad? Something that other, keener Christians do? Something you support financially?

Read Luke 10:1-20

This passage is similar to when Jesus sent his twelve disciples out in 9:1-6. But there, he was sending those who would become his apostles, a role we will never have. Here, he sends 72 ordinary followers of his—a role we, if we're Christians, already have.

Ask and go

❷ *As Jesus looks out at the world, what problem does he see (10:2)?*
❷ *What should Christians do about this?*

Beware: this is a dangerous thing to do—it might be that *you* are the answer to your prayer! Jesus calls his people not only to ask (v 2) but also to "Go!" (v 3). And he does not promise it will be easy—we will be like "lambs among wolves" (v 3). Mission often meets with mockery, rejection or worse. Our Lord never pretended otherwise—but still he tells us to "Go!"

All Christians are missionaries, enjoying the rather terrifying privilege of being sent by Jesus. In your workplace, at the school gates, out with friends, at a family gathering… Jesus has sent you there to serve and speak for him. That's your corner of the harvest field.

Welcome and woe

❷ *What responses will they experience as they go on mission (v 8-11)?*

Sodom was a city infamous for its horrific sin, and God's terrifying judgment (see Genesis 19:1-9, 27-29).

❷ *Why is rejecting Jesus' messengers a serious thing to do (Luke 10:11-16)?*

True joy

❷ *What prompts joy in the seventy-two?*

Jesus agrees that his coming marks Satan's fall (v 18).

❷ *Where should they find most joy (v 20)?*

Jesus has saved us from Satan and hell. This should cause us to rejoice! And it should be part of our message to a world still in slavery to Satan. But Jesus has saved us for something too—for life in eternity. This should make us rejoice still more! And it should be an essential part of our message to a world searching for "life" in the wrong places.

☑ Apply

❷ *Where do you find most joy in life? Do you need to think more about your eternal destiny?*
❷ *Are you praying about the harvest field? Why not research a particular country, and commit to praying for Jesus' work there?*
❷ *Which bits of the harvest field has Jesus called you to work in? Do you do it faithfully?*

God is in charge

To be honest, I find the prospect of telling others terrifying. Today, Jesus gives us three great encouragements to be his "missionary-messengers" where he has placed us.

God reveals

Read Luke 10:21

Here, we're getting a brief glimpse into the life of the Trinity, as the Spirit-inspired Son speaks to the Father.

> ❷ *What does Jesus praise the Father for?*
> ❷ *Who does God reveal himself to be?*

Human reason only goes so far—and it can never work out the mind of God. The most intelligent people often have the least idea about who God is and what he is like—and the smallest child often has much to teach us about real faith in God. This is no accident—it is how God has decided to work in his world. It keeps us humble. It keeps us grateful.

☑ Apply

> ❷ *In what ways can churches prize intellectual ability above heartfelt faith?*

The Son chooses

Read Luke 10:22

> ❷ *How can anyone know who God the Father and God the Son are?*

At first sight, this might seem to dissuade us from telling people about Jesus. Since the only way anyone can know the Lord is if he chooses to reveal himself to them, what's the point of telling others?

But we saw yesterday that the way people come to know Jesus is through his people telling them. That's the way the Son reveals himself—through our mission. This keeps us prayerful—our words alone will never bring someone to faith. This keeps us witnessing—our words can be used by Jesus to bring anyone to faith.

Jesus can bring people to faith in him any way he chooses. And he chooses—us! He chooses to work through lambs among wolves, through you and me. What a privilege!

☑ Apply

Is there someone you know who you feel will never come to trust Jesus? Start asking Jesus to choose to reveal himself to them. And start looking for ways to speak to them about him.

We are blessed

Read Luke 10:23-24

Ever wished you could have known God as Moses did, or David, or Elijah? You know God more than they did—because you know him through Jesus, by his Spirit. If we come to appreciate that blessing more ourselves, we'll come to share that blessing more with others—whatever the response they give us. Praise God!

What must I do?

The next parable is possibly the most well known of them all—and possibly one of the most misunderstood.

To get the parable's real point, we need to see the context. Luke pairs this conversation with another, which we'll see tomorrow. Together, they answer the question: "What must I do to inherit eternal life?"

The religious expert
Read Luke 10:25-28

> ❓ *Why did this man decide to ask Jesus a question (v 25)?*

Throughout the Gospels, when someone asks Jesus something with this motivation, they often find themselves without a full answer. Here, Jesus, as he so often does, asks a question in reply (v 26).

> ❓ *How does the expert sum up the Law, and what does Jesus make of his reply?*

It's all quite simple: if we love God with all that we are, and love the people he's made with all that we have, then we will have done enough to have eternal life.

The good Samaritan
Read Luke 10:29-37

> ❓ *What motivates the question (v 29)?*

It's the natural response to hearing that we need to love God and love our neighbour to get eternal life: *Am I doing well enough?* The expert needs to know who counts as his neighbour, so he can see if his life is sufficiently good. So Jesus tells his famous parable. Samaritans were hated by the Jews—

we need to feel the shock of the Lord's use of a Samaritan in his story.

> ❓ *What are the surprises in the parable?*
> ❓ *How does it answer the question?*

The cliffhanger

> ❓ *What is the challenge for the questioner?*

Jesus is answering the expert's question in its own terms. The dominant word all the way through is *do*: "What must I *do* to inherit eternal life?" (v 25); "*Do* this and you will live (v 28); "Go and *do* likewise" (v 37).

This is not a story primarily about how to live with your neighbour (though that doesn't mean we can ignore Jesus' command to love others like this). It's a story about the standard required to earn eternal life. The challenge is: have we always acted towards everyone else as the Samaritan does in the parable? And that's before we ask whether we have always loved God with everything we are.

Jesus' answer to the question in verse 25 is: more than you could ever manage.

⌄ Apply

The expert's assumption is still popular.

> ❓ *Do you ever catch yourself thinking what you do is enough to deserve eternal life?*
> ❓ *How would you explain the real teaching of this parable to a friend?*

God my exceeding joy

There's a huge difference between naïve optimism and confidence in God.

Read Psalms 42 – 43

Our writer feels like a lone voice crying out in the wilderness of his people's unbelief.

Feeling misjudged

Read Psalm 43:1

A recurring theme in the Book of Psalms is the godly one standing out among an ungodly people, for whom deceit and injustice are simply the means to promote their own interests. They've abandoned God and are offended by our psalmist's refusal to join them. But he still has what they've discarded as worthless: he knows God will finally vindicate him.

Feeling abandoned

Read Psalm 43:2

Although he knows the truths he declares, he feels abandoned by God. Yet he knows God hasn't changed, so despite his subjective feelings, he clings to objective knowledge of God, and calls on him, knowing there's nowhere else to go.

❷ *Will you bring your hard questions and problems to God?*
❷ *Are you committed to knowing him as he shows himself to us in Scripture?*

Feeling hope

Read Psalm 43:3-4

Holding on to God finally pays off. Our psalmist has given himself a thorough talking-to, remembering what he already knows, and now his spirit lifts. He comes confidently to God, knowing the light and truth of his word are a sufficient guide to lead him back into knowing and rejoicing in God's presence. He worships God with all his heart, despite his circumstances, because God is always available.

Old-covenant believers approached God at the Jerusalem Temple. Christians come to God in Christ, and can never be cut off by geography or human malice. We know him who has said, "Never will I leave you; never will I forsake you" (Hebrews 13:5).

❷ *Is your worship driven by knowing God, or seeking a feeling of wellbeing or excitement?*
❷ *Can you worship God, even when you don't "feel it"?*

Chorus

Read Psalm 43:5

If you're feeling fine, prepare for when you won't be, by memorising this verse and meditating on the truths of this pair of psalms.

If you're feeling like our psalmist, take courage and comfort from the truths he's proclaimed to you.

Who must I know?

The parable of the good Samaritan leaves us with a problem: how can we possibly do enough to have eternal life? As we follow Jesus into the home of some friends, we discover the answer: it's not about what you do.

Martha

Read Luke 10:38-40

❓ *What is good about what Martha does?*

❓ *What do you make of her complaint? Does she have a point, do you think?*

Martha's a do-er. And so would many of us be, in her position. God's chosen all-powerful King, Jesus, has picked her house to eat in and stay in. Of course she was "distracted by all the preparations that had to be made" (v 40)!

Mary

❓ *What does Mary do, which so annoys Martha (v 40)?*

❓ *What does Martha want Jesus to command Mary to do?*

Jesus

Read Luke 10:41-42

❓ *What does Jesus say Martha has forgotten?*

❓ *What is it that Mary "has chosen", which is "better" (v 39, 42)?*

It's what Mary has, and Martha lacks, that "will not be taken away"—that will last to eternity. Here's the answer to the expert's question back in verse 25. Both he, and Martha, are focused on what they *do*. And what they do is good—helping their neighbour, working for Jesus. But focusing on what we do has two huge problems:

- We can never do enough to earn eternal life.
- It can easily and unnoticeably draw us away from spending time with Jesus.

Ultimately, what matters for eternal life is *not* what we do, but *who we know*. It's a living relationship with Jesus which is the one thing needed (v 42).

⌄ Apply

How can you tell if you're a Martha, rather than a Mary?

- If you have a busy day, you drop your Bible and prayer time, rather than something else.
- You get both proud and annoyed about the fact you do more for your church than other members do.

So it's worth doing some self-diagnosis.

❓ *How are you, or how could you be, Martha-ish? What do you need to change in your attitude or your routines to make sure you're a Mary?*

⌃ Pray

Speak to the Lord now. Thank him for your relationship with him. Pray that your service of him would never stop you spending time with him; and pray that you would never think you need to earn the eternal life he's given to those who know him.

We call him Father

Most people pray at some stage in their lives—and Christians certainly do. Yet often people find they're not quite sure what they should say. We need someone to "teach us to pray" (v 1)—and who better than the Son of God?

Prayer
Read Luke 11:1-4

Jesus' "model prayer" here isn't just to be repeated word for word: it's an outline to help us structure our personal praying.

> ❷ *What is amazing about how Christians address the almighty Creator of the universe (v 2)?*

There's a wonderful photograph of US President John F Kennedy sitting working at his desk in the White House; the most powerful seat in the world. Underneath the desk sits his young son. No other boy had such instant access to the president. No other boy could call this man "Dad". How amazing to have such a father!

When we as Christians pray, we enter heaven's throne room; we sit at the feet of the most powerful, most perfect one in the universe. And we call Him "Father"! Pause a moment and drink in that truth.

> ❷ *How does it make you feel?*

Verse 3 is telling us to ask God to supply what we need materially each day. We're normally pretty good at doing this!

⌄ Apply
> ❷ *What should we be praying for first (v 2)?*
> ❷ *And what else do we need to ask for (v 4)?*
> ❷ *We call God "Father"! How would appreciating this more change your praying?*

> ❷ *Look again at the content of Jesus' model prayer. Do you need to add to, or change, what you ask God for each day?*

Persistence
Read Luke 11:5-8

> ❷ *What does the "friend" of verse 5 end up doing, and why (v 8)?*

Often we struggle to pray because we think God won't listen or he can't help. When we feel like that, we need to remember that, like the friend, God will listen to and act for those who ask. Yet how often "you do not have, because you do not ask God" (James 4:2)!

Promise
Read Luke 11:9-13

A good but flawed human father gives his children the good things they ask for (v 11-12). How much more will our perfect, flawless heavenly Father! Above all, he gives us his Spirit, to keep us loving him, to change us to be like him, to bring us safely home to him. What a Father!

⌃ Pray

Use verses 2-4 to shape your prayers now, and each day, as you speak to your Father.

Victor and King

On 6th June 1944—D-Day—Allied troops landed in northern France to begin the liberation of occupied Europe. It was a re-invasion; and the German armies were forced to retreat until their final defeat almost a year later.

In AD 0 (*ish!*), another re-invasion of this world began...

Defeating the enemy
Read Luke 11:14-22

❓ *What responses do we see to the miracle of verse 14 (v 14-16)?*

The reaction in verse 16 is clearly ridiculous. These people have just watched a miracle, and they say: "Show us a miracle"!

❓ *Why does Jesus say the reaction in verse 15 is ridiculous, too (v 17-18)?*

Thinking Jesus drives demons out because he's working for Satan is like thinking the Allied troops were working for Hitler on D-Day!

❓ *Where does Jesus say his power does come from (v 20)?*
❓ *And what do his miracles show (v 20-22)?*

By nature, we are the "possessions" (v 21) of Satan. In convincing us to sin, he brings us under his power and drags us down to hell. And he is too strong for us to fight. He has invaded and occupied our hearts, our lives and our futures.

❓ *Why is the arrival of "someone stronger", Jesus, such good news (v 22)?*

···· **TIME OUT** ··································
Read Genesis 3:1-6, 14-15

❓ *How is Jesus the fulfilment of God's promise in verse 15?*
Read Colossians 2:15

In dying, Jesus' "heel" was struck by the devil. The devil's greatest weapon is death, and he seemed to have triumphed as God's Son died. But in dying our death, in our place, Jesus crushed the devil. Satan's greatest weapon has been emptied of ammunition. He has nothing more to throw at us. He is defeated.

Following the King
Read Luke 11:23-28

Coming into contact with Jesus, or his church, often helps people to put their lives "in order" (v 25)—helped through grief, or freed from slavery to sin, or released from loneliness. But Jesus warns that simply enjoying those benefits leaves people in a dangerous position. It's only hearing God's word and obeying it (v 28)—only following Jesus as Lord and Rescuer—which leads to real life, the blessed life.

⌄ Apply

The only weapon the devil has left is lies—telling Christians they can't be forgiven this time, or that sin is a good idea.

❓ *In what areas of your life is the devil regularly lying to you?*

Jesus and Jonah

Later in the Gospel of Luke, we'll see Jesus telling his friends "what was said in all the Scriptures concerning himself" (24:27). Here, Jesus takes two Old Tesament events and uses them to explain both the shape of his ministry and the only right response to him.

Read Luke 11:29-32

The sign of Jonah

❓ *How does Jesus describe his listeners, and why (v 29)?*

❓ *What is the only "sign" they will see (v 29)?*

Jesus links himself, the Son of Man, with Jonah.

❓ *How did Nineveh respond when Jonah preached to them (v 32)?*

Read Matthew 12:39-40

❓ *What had happened to Jonah that was evidence that he was God's prophet?*

❓ *What event in Jesus' ministry is the ultimate "sign" that he is God's Christ?*

There is no excuse for not repenting. Christ's cross and empty tomb are all the proof anyone needs that what he says about our sin, God's judgment, and our need to turn back to him is true. When God judges every human, the repentant Ninevites will say to anyone who heard about Jesus' resurrection, and then asked for more evidence: *You fools* (Luke 11:32).

▼ Apply

Jesus warns us not to base our faith on impressive signs, nor on intellectual reasoning or emotive feelings. He points us to his cross, tomb and resurrection. That is the firm foundation of the Christian faith. That is where we are to base our confidence in him. All else—our thoughts, our feelings, our experiences—is shifting sand.

❓ *How should this shape the way you encourage struggling Christians?*

❓ *How will this shape the way you talk about your faith with those who don't know Jesus?*

Queen of the South

Solomon was the king of Israel at its peak. And the Queen of the South—powerful and wealthy though she was—was humble enough to realize that this was God's king, to listen to him, and to worship his God (1 Kings 10:1-10). She, too, will look at Jesus' hearers on judgment day and "condemn them" (Luke 11:31). Why? Because she listened to Solomon, and "now something greater than Solomon is here".

◤ Pray

Thank God for the "sign of Jonah"— the death, burial and resurrection of Jesus. Thank him for the certainty you find in that sign. Pray that it would always be enough for you—and that it would be what you point others to.

Lighting-up time

The antagonism between Jesus and his opponents is ratcheting up, notch by notch. We've reached a stage where they're accusing him of working for the devil (11:15)— and where Jesus is accusing them of being "a wicked generation" (v 29).

How will God's chosen King respond to living in a society increasingly opposed to him? And how should his followers live in such a society, then and today?

What to do with light

Read Luke 11:33

> ❷ *What don't you do with a lamp?*
> ❷ *Why not?*

"Light" is Jesus' image here for his person and his teaching.

> ❷ *What's he saying he won't do? Why not?*

Verse 33 may be ringing a bell! That's because Jesus has already said this (look back to 8:16).

> ❷ *Why do you think he repeats this teaching?*

···· **TIME OUT** ·····································

Jesus was under pressure to withdraw from public ministry. It can't have been easy to continue to preach and teach a crowd who demanded more evidence (11:16), or said he was devilish (v 15).

Christians today are under increasing pressure to withdraw from the public arena. Faith is, we're told, a private matter—fine for the home, but not to be spoken of or lived by in the workplace or the street. Christians in the public eye are mocked if they admit to praying for guidance, or believing in the resurrection, or wanting to abide by biblical standards of sexual morality.

> ❷ *How does verse 33 speak to us today?*

What to do with eyes

Jesus keeps using the imagery of light, but now he's moving on to make a different point.

Read Luke 11:34-36

> ❷ *Why does it matter what our eyes look at (v 33-34)?*
> ❷ *What do we need to make sure about our eyes (v 35)?*

Jesus is the light. We need to make sure our eyes are being lit up by looking at him. As the moon reflects the sun's rays onto the earth, so our eyes must be reflecting Jesus' words to the rest of our body.

▾ Apply

Now, as then, this is a dark world, full of ideas and images which are opposed to Jesus' teaching.

> ❷ *What do your eyes look at which is unhelpful to you as a Christian? Do you need to ask God to enable you to stop looking at a particular magazine, or website, or person?*
> ❷ *How often do your eyes look at Jesus' words in the Bible? How could you make sure your eyes see Jesus' words throughout the day?*

An uncomfortable dinner

Inviting Jesus for dinner was risky. You never knew who would turn up (7:36-50); and you never knew what he'd say...

Read Luke 11:37-54

Inside, outside

❓ *As Jesus begins to eat, what does the Pharisee who's invited him notice (v 38)?*

The Jewish religious leaders demanded, and kept, a very high standard of external cleanliness. It was part of what they believed made them acceptable to God.

❓ *But what is the problem (v 39-41)?*

Rules-based religion, like what we see here, is focused on performance, on the externals. It is motivated by greed—our own desire to gain favour from God. And it is a blanket for wickedness—a "good" life can hide many heart-sins.

Christ-centred faith, on the other hand, is focused on the heart, on our need for him to clean us internally. And (as Jesus implies in verse 41) it is motivated by generosity—we have received life from God, so we are free to give all we are and have to others, in his service and for their sake. Christ-centred faith admits wickedness, thanks him for dying to forgive it, and asks his Spirit to remove it.

Six woes

And in fact, the internal uncleanliness of these religious leaders has led them to a series of unclean behaviours anyway.

❓ *What are the six "woes" (actions which earn God's judgment)?*
❓ *What do you understand Jesus to be saying in each of them?*

They should know better. God's consistent message, in Old and New Testament times, is: "I desire ... acknowledgement of God rather than burnt offerings" (Hosea 6:6). Internal attitude must match, and inspire, outward performance. But those who prefer rules-based religion simply ignore, persecute and kill those who teach this truth (Luke 11:48-49).

The real tragedy comes in verse 52. These teachers are missing out on having life with God through Christ—they're also blocking others who are considering coming to him. They're standing at the door to relationship with God and saying: *Don't go in.* Woe!

⌄ Apply

Have a good look inside yourself.

❓ *What do you think makes you right with God? Jesus' performance, or yours? What Jesus has done for you, or what you do for Jesus?*
❓ *Are you using outward respectability to hide or excuse a deep-rooted sin? Will you admit it, beg for forgiveness, and ask to be changed?*

Confused by setbacks

We know that Jesus won the victory for all time on the cross. We've read/heard of God doing amazing things for some Christians in mission or ministry. It's easy to assume that the advance of the gospel is normal and normative.

Then: glory days

Read Psalm 44:1-8

If this were the whole of the psalm, we'd think it was a song of God's victory, correctly attributing Israel's victories in battle to him.

> ❓ *What has God done for his people, according to our psalmist?*
> ❓ *What hint is there that all is not well?*

Now: inglorious days

Read Psalm 44:9-22

Although our psalmist thinks he knows how things should be, the setbacks his nation faces on every side contradict him.

> ❓ *Can you see situations in the world that seem to contradict what you know about God's character and purposes?*

···· TIME OUT ·······································

We live in a fallen world, broken by sin.

Read Romans 8:18-25; Hebrews 12:3-13

> ❓ *How does this help us to see setbacks differently?*
> ❓ *How does God use adverse circumstances for our benefit?*

Some Christians suggest that setbacks and difficulties in life are specific and negative judgments of God on particular sins and failings.

> ❓ *Why is this an inadequate account of reality?*

There is a type of church where the so-called "prosperity gospel" is promoted. It uses slogans like, "Name it and claim it," or "Living in victory," and claims that "God's will is for you to be healthy and wealthy". It is pernicious because people's faith is damaged when events seem to turn against them.

Jesus himself perfectly obeyed his Father's will in all things, yet he was arrested. Although he had committed no crime, tried without due process of law, tortured for the amusement of his guards, then nailed to a cross to be killed. If prosperity theology were true, none of that should have happened.

An anguished appeal

Read Psalm 44:23-26

We might expect our psalmist to stop trusting God in the face of all that. But although he may not understand what God is doing, yet he keeps on addressing his prayers to God. His faith is stronger than a few setbacks can destroy.

◤ Pray

Ask God to keep you trusting him, no matter what happens. Pray for anyone you know whose faith is being tested by adverse circumstances.

What do you fear?

What we most fear will direct our decisions and actions in life. As you look at your present and future circumstances, what are you most afraid of? What do you think you should be most afraid of?

Don't be afraid

Read Luke 12:1-4

Jesus knows his opponents' anger will one day turn to violence towards him and his followers (v 4).

> ❷ *So what's strange about his command in verse 4 ?*
> ❷ *What reasons does he give for this (v 2-4)?*

Be afraid

Read Luke 12:5

> ❷ *Who should Jesus' followers fear, and why (v 5)?*

The worst any human can do is kill you! But God has the power to do much worse to those who stand against him. Hell is a reality beyond death that we should be terrified of facing.

But don't be afraid

Luke 12:6-12

Jesus has told us to fear God (v 5)—then immediately tells us we don't need to be afraid (v 7)! And he gives three reasons why those who follow him even in hard times don't need to fear the God who can "throw you into hell" (v 5). The first is that God knows, remembers and values his people (v 6-7).

> ❷ *What's the second (v 8-9)?*

❷ *What's the third (v 11-12)?*

In the Garden of Eden, the first sinful man told God he'd hidden from him because "[He] was afraid" (Genesis 3:10). Terror at the prospect of meeting God goes hand in hand with rebelling against God—and so by nature we should live in fear of him. But in his great love for his people, God has done two things:

- *He has secured our future.* When judgment comes, those who stood up for his Son in life will find his Son standing up for them beyond death (Luke 12:8).

- *He will support our present.* Whatever the world does, those who stand up for God's Son will find his Spirit giving them all they need (v 12).

TIME OUT

What is verse 10 saying?! The context suggests Jesus is warning that a lifelong refusal to accept him as the Spirit-filled Son of God will not be forgiven beyond death. Christians can't commit this sin!

⌄ Apply

> ❷ *How has this passage encouraged you?*
> ❷ *How does it challenge you?*
> ❷ *Is there a recent situation in which you've been afraid of standing up for Jesus? What will you do differently next time?*

You fool!

Most disagreements within families are about money. Financial squabbles can cause simmering resentment, or boil over into mutual hatred. It's a family row over inheritance money that Jesus is asked to intervene in here.

Rich?

Read Luke 12:13-21

- ❓ *Where is the man in Jesus' parable looking for security for his future?*
- ❓ *Where does he think his satisfaction will come from (v 19)?*
- ❓ *How many times does he say "I" and "my"? What does this tell us about his focus?*

Jesus told this parable about a society 2,000 years ago. But it is perhaps even more relevant today.

- ❓ *How does the attitude of the man in the parable show itself in your culture?*
- ❓ *Do you see it in yourself at all?*

Not rich

- ❓ *Why is this man a "fool" (v 20)?*
- ❓ *Jesus is warning against focusing on material gain in life. What should people focus on instead (v 21)?*
- ❓ *Imagine the man in the parable had done as Jesus advises. When he "produced a good crop", how would his thinking and his actions have been different?*

The real sting comes at the beginning. The man asking the question (v 13) hasn't reached the extremes of the man in the parable. He's just trying to settle a family inheritance dispute. But Jesus looks under the surface. He doesn't help the man deal with the issue: he helps him to look at the attitude in his heart.

- ❓ *What attitude must he be aware of (v 15)?*

"Possession-itis" is a common disease in wealthy societies. Billboards, adverts, the neighbours, our own hearts, all prompt us to think: "If I just had this, or that, or the other—then I would be satisfied, then I'd feel secure". We are regular worshippers of a god called "Just-a-bit-more".

It's a god who doesn't deliver. Most people who have great wealth realise in life that money doesn't buy happiness; *every* person will see that in death, as they leave behind all they've worked to gain.

We must, though, beware the opposite danger of finding security in thrift. Being "rich towards God"—giving all we are to him, and finding our security and satisfaction in him—is the cure to greed.

▼ Apply

We're much better at spotting greed in others than in ourselves!

- ❓ *How do you need to "watch out" for greed in your own life?*
- ❓ *When in particular do you need to remember to find security and satisfaction in living for God?*

A command, not a request

Here's a clear command from Jesus that we often downgrade to a request, or an unrealistic idea.

Read Luke 12:22-31

❓ *What's the three-word command (v 22)?*

Almost everyone worries from time to time. Many people worry all the time! It's worth asking: why? Usually it's because:

- we think something is in our control (exams, or parenting, or an interview)—so we worry about getting it wrong.
- we know something is out of our control (pandemics, illness, having children, unemployment)—so we worry because there's nothing we can do.

❓ *What are you worrying about today? Can you put your finger on why?*

Worry doesn't work

❓ *What should we not worry about (v 22)?*

Many of us don't need to worry about these things—we already have them! But that doesn't stop us worrying—we simply find something else to worry about.

❓ *But what does Jesus point out about worrying (v 25-26)?*

Worry isn't needed

❓ *What truth does Jesus point to (v 30)?*
❓ *What examples from creation does he point to (v 24, 27, 28)?*

When we worry, we are seeking security in something other than God. We are relying on ourselves, or on a particular possession or circumstance. When we worry, we are not relying on God.

❓ *What should we replace our worry with (v 31)?*

It's very easy to spend life worrying about getting or keeping the things of this world—and only if we have some spare time or emotion do we think about living with God as King. The antidote to worry is to switch the two around. Our role is to seek to live God's way in every situation—and to leave the rest to him.

How to stop worrying
Read Luke 12:32-34

❓ *What do Christians already have (v 32)?*
❓ *What should we do (v 33)? How is this attitude the opposite of the rich fool Jesus introduced us to yesterday (v 16-20)?*

If you're a habitual worrier, Jesus tells you how you can begin to change your heart from self-reliance to God-reliance. Take a possession you think you need, and give it away. Show yourself you need nothing but God, and the place he's given you in his eternal kingdom.

Pray

❓ *What do you need to give control of to God, asking him to help you rely on him?*

Ready?

Interviews… exams… holidays… Christmas… We spend our lives getting ready for things. Our knowledge of what is coming in the future directs our behaviour in the present.

Be ready
Read Luke 12:35-40

> ❓ *What do we know about the future? What don't we know (v 40)?*
> ❓ *How should we respond to this knowledge (v 40)?*

In Jesus' parable of verses 35-38, the master is a picture of himself.

> ❓ *What awaits those who are ready for Jesus to return (v 37)?*
> ❓ *Why is this exciting?*

It's a simple message: be ready for Jesus' return, since it could be today. Just as the only way to be prepared for a thief's entrance into your house is to be ready all the time (v 39), so the only way to be prepared for the Lord's entrance into his world is to be in a constant state of readiness.

✅ Apply

> ❓ *How often do you think about the Lord's return?*
> ❓ *How does knowing he will return shape the way you think and act?*
> ❓ *If you had believed Jesus could come at any time, what would you have done differently yesterday?*

Show you're ready
Read Luke 12:41-48

Peter asks whether this parable is directed at Jesus' followers, or at the interested crowds. While verses 35-40 seem to be for everyone, the Lord's answer to Peter's question appears to be for those who consider themselves part of his people, to encourage and challenge them to *show* that they are ready for his return.

> ❓ *What does the master ask the manager to do while he is away (v 42)?*
> ❓ *What two options does the manager ("that servant", v 43) have?*
> ❓ *What are the outcomes (v 43-44, v 46)?*

If we know Jesus is returning, we will show our readiness by looking after his people (the other servants of v 42), encouraging and helping them to keep being ready, in whatever way he has given us. It may be pastoring a congregation. Or helping in a children's group. Or talking to a friend over coffee. Or praying for a member of your church.

But we will always face the temptation to ignore those opportunities and instead to make life easier or more fun for ourselves. And the warning of verse 46 is stark.

✅ Apply

> ❓ *What ways has the Lord given you to look after his people? Is your motivation for doing those tasks other-centred, or self-centred?*

Our era

We live in the 21st century; in the internet age; in the postmodern era; in the time of Joe Biden, Vladimir Putin and Li Keqiang. But, much more importantly, we live between two massive markers in time…

Past

Read Luke 12:49-50

❓ *What does Jesus say he's come to bring (v 49)?*

Read 2 Peter 3:7, 12-13

❓ *What is the "fire" that is coming to the world?*

It's striking that Jesus is looking forward to this day—in fact, during his time on earth, he wished it had already begun (Luke 12:49). The day when sin is judged and punished, so that the world can be restored to perfection, is a day Jesus longs for. *Do we?*

Future

❓ *What must happen before the "fire" of judgment day (v 50)?*

This is an image Jesus used to talk about his death. Our baptism is a *picture* of God's judgment in death before the resurrection of new life (Romans 6:3-4)—but Jesus faced the *real thing*. He knew that before he returned to bring the fire of destruction and recreation, he must face judgment on the cross so that his people could pass through the "kindled" fire and into his kingdom.

🔼 Pray

Throughout his ministry, Jesus knew where he was headed—and that the full force of

God's judgment on our sin would fall on him. Yet he still walked towards the cross. Praise and thank him for his love for you.

Present

Read Luke 12:51-59

Jesus goes on to explain what life will be like between the cross and the judgment.

❓ *What will, and won't, there be (v 51)?*

The world, even families, will be divided between those who follow Jesus, and those who don't (v 52). And that's the only division which remains eternally.

Yet though the people of Jesus' day could look at the sky and predict the weather, the great majority of them couldn't "interpret [the] present time" (v 56). We may put up an umbrella when the sky turns black—but do we see Jesus' return on the horizon of the future and stay prepared for it?

Jesus finishes by picturing God as our adversary.

❓ *Since the world is "on the way" towards judgment, what do we all desperately need to do (v 58)? Why (v 58-59)?*

🔽 Apply

❓ *How will knowing you live between the cross and the judgment change the way you think, feel and act today?*

Dealing with news of death

We live in a culture that has avoided the reality and the mention of death—until a global pandemic brought us face to face with it. How should we respond when death comes uncomfortably close?

God's megaphone

Read Luke 13:1-5

> ❓ *What two events are in focus (v 1, 4)?*
> ❓ *What did people think caused them (v 2, 4)?*
> ❓ *Were they right, according to Jesus (v 3, 5)?*

It's important to see that Jesus isn't saying those who died were not sinful or guilty. His point is that they were no *more* sinful than any of the people listening to him. They had not done anything to deserve that particular death—but as sinners, they had done everything to deserve death itself. So have his listeners.

Jesus doesn't want us to ponder *how* or *when* we'll die: but he does want us to realise we *will* die. When we are confronted by another's mortality, Jesus encourages us to look to our own. Death is God's megaphone to a deaf world. It reminds us that, despite all our technological and medical know-how, all is not well with this world. We die.

> ❓ *So how should people respond to hearing about death (v 3, 5)?*

If we die while turned away from God, death is a dead end. If we turn back to God before our days are over, we discover that death is a doorway to life with him.

God's calendar

Read Luke 13:6-9

Scripture often uses the fig tree and the vineyard as pictures of Israel (see Isaiah 5:2; Hosea 9:10). In this parable, the man of Luke 13:6 represents God.

> ❓ *What does Jesus mean when he says the man "did not find any" fruit (v 6)?*
> ❓ *What does he threaten to do (v 7)?*
> ❓ *How is the parable a warning?*

God "is patient with you, not wanting anyone to perish, but everyone to come to repentance" (2 Peter 3:9). And yet "he has set a day when he will judge the world with justice" (Acts 17:31). Both our deaths and the return of God's Son mean it is crucial, and urgent, that we repent—and go on repenting throughout our lives.

> ❓ *How can Jesus' words here help us to respond to non-Christians next time there is a natural disaster?*

☑ Apply

> ❓ *Have you accepted the certainty of death, and given your life to God and trusted him to bring you through it?*
> ❓ *Do you seek to warn others about judgment, and urge them to repent while there is still time, as Jesus does here? Who should you pray for?*

Bible in a year: Jeremiah 51-52 • Philippians 3

A love song for you

The whole Old Testament, including the Psalms, points us forward to Jesus. Today's song makes that abundantly clear.

❓ *How do you see yourself? If you had to come up with three words to describe yourself, what would they be?*

❓ *What three words do you think Jesus might use of you?*

Love song for the king

Read Psalm 45:1

Probably composed for the marriage of a king of Judah, it begins with a dedication. But although its writer couldn't have known, God inspired him to point us forward to the end of history, Christ's return, and John's vision in Revelation of the marriage feast of the Lamb (see Ephesians 5:25-33; Revelation 19:6-8).

❓ *What's the state of the writer's heart?*

His joy in relating the king's wedding is a pale shadow of the joy to be revealed when Jesus comes for his bride.

The anointed King

Read Psalm 45:2-9

Within the flattery, the writer tells his vision of the ideal king. His outward appearance and inward qualities (revealed in actions) are attractive. King Jesus protects his people by his glory. Read these verses again, seeing Jesus where the writer addresses his king.

❓ *Flattery is insincere and untruthful praise. Is it possible to flatter Jesus?*

Jesus has already given his life for his bride. He will return, as King and Judge. Those who will not submit to him now in loving obedience, will submit then as defeated enemies.

❓ *Which of those will you be?*

The king was anointed and given special clothing, as were the priests, who mediated the nation's relationship with God through the sacrificial temple worship. The Messiah is both King, Priest, and Bridegroom.

❓ *Is anything too much to give for Jesus, your King, Priest and Bridegroom?*

The chosen bride

Read Psalm 45:10-17

The earthly setting points to Jesus, coming to claim his bride—the church—you and me, all who love and serve him. Just as the king's bride must leave her former life behind, so to belong to Christ is to put aside everything belonging to our earthly life; to put him in first place, before all other relationships. As the king embraces the princess in his wedding joy, Jesus embraces us, knowing what we one day shall be.

❓ *Do you look forward to your marriage made in heaven, full of divine joy, beauty, grace and fruitfulness?*

❓ *Now answer the first two questions in light of what you have read, and pray about your answers.*

The Sabbath fight

Of the battles Jesus and his opponents contested, few were more regularly and fiercely disputed than the Sabbath. There've been two fights already (6:1-11)—here's the third.

The battleground
Read Deuteronomy 5:12-15

- ❷ *What is different about the Sabbath (v 13-14)?*
- ❷ *Where should the focus be on this day (v 15)?*

Until the cross, the exodus from Egypt was the place God's people looked back on to remember that God is a rescuing God, who saves his people from evil and brings them the blessings of life spent enjoying and obeying him. God's people needed to be reminded that their efforts hadn't saved them; God's power had. The Sabbath was a chance to stop *their* work, to remember that they relied on *God's* work.

The spark
Read Luke 13:10-13

- ❷ *What does Jesus do (v 11-13)?*
- ❷ *How does she respond (v 13)?*
- ❷ *How is this picturing the same truth about God that the exodus did?*
- ❷ *Why is it fitting that Jesus, God on Earth, did this on a Sabbath?*

The attack
Read Luke 13:14

The synagogue ruler doesn't think it's fitting at all! His response here would be hilarious if it weren't so offensive. He tells anyone else who needs salvation from evil to seek it during the working week!

The counter-attack
Read Luke 13:15-17

- ❷ *How does Jesus respond (v 15-16)?*

His opponent has got the Sabbath all wrong in two ways. First, he actually isn't resting— he's not acknowledging he needs God to rely on God, not himself (v 15). And second, he's forgotten that the Sabbath is a day to remember that God works to save people— as he has just seen in front of his eyes!

- ❷ *How do they react to Jesus (v 13, 14, 17)?*

⌄ Apply

It's easy to shake our heads at the synagogue ruler. We wouldn't argue about the Sabbath like that! But we may share his underlying problem. When our assumptions or understanding or lifestyle or traditions are challenged by Jesus, what do we do? Do we get annoyed with him? Ignore him? Or remember that he is the saving God, who has saved us to obey him, rely on him, and be blessed by him?

⌃ Pray

Thank God that he has rescued you from evil. Ask him to enable you to be humble enough to change and obey.

Not like Coke

We live in the day of the corporation. Global market share is what counts—and it's gained through bold slogans and great marketing. Then there's the kingdom of God…

As we've followed Jesus through the pages of Luke, we've been given glimpses of his kingdom—and we've been invited to join it through living with him as our King. But if Jesus is the King, and the kingdom of God is so amazing, why is the kingdom not like Apple, Coke or Nike—big, successful, all-conquering? What has been going on for the 2,000 years between the time Jesus came to establish the kingdom and the time we live in?

Read Luke 13:18-21

Mustard seed

Jesus compares the kingdom to a tiny mustard seed (v 19).

- ❷ *Though it starts small, what does the seed become (v 19)?*
- ❷ *By using this comparison, what is Jesus telling us about God's kingdom?*

The "birds of the air" is a picture of the world's nations (see Ezekiel 17:22-24).

- ❷ *Why is the end of Luke 13:19 exciting for those of us who are not part of Israel?*

Yeast

- ❷ *What happens to the yeast (v 21)?*
- ❷ *What is Jesus telling us about God's kingdom?*

In the first picture, the kingdom is like a man planting a seed in his garden—Jesus, coming to his world at a particular point in history to begin the growth of his kingdom, before returning to heaven. In the second, the kingdom is like a woman working at spreading yeast through dough. Again, it's a picture of Jesus, working by his Spirit throughout history to continue the growth of his kingdom, before returning from heaven.

Jesus is in charge both of the start and the spread of the kingdom of God. And, like a growing seed or yeast introduced into dough, the kingdom's progress is irreversible and unstoppable.

⌄ Apply

- ❷ *Jesus' contemporaries expected the kingdom to come suddenly and decisively. How do Jesus' comparisons challenge their view?*
- ❷ *Today, we can want the kingdom to come impressively and obviously. How does Jesus challenge this view?*

⌃ Pray

Thank Jesus that his kingdom grows—gradually, unseen, unstoppably. Thank him that he is sovereign over his kingdom and his world. Ask him to give you the privilege of being part of the way he works it throughout the dough of this world.

No room for complacency

A friend of mine thinks he'll go to heaven (if it exists—he's not sure) because he is (a) British and (b) baptised. Many people assume that most people will be saved.

In Jesus' day, most Jews assumed that all Jews would be saved. And here, Jesus wants to challenge that kind of comfortable complacency.

Read Luke 13:22-30

Pleading

❓ *What's the question (v 23)?*
❓ *What's the warning (v 24)?*
❓ *On what basis do people think they're saved (v 26)?*
❓ *On what basis will Jesus shut them out of heaven (v 25, 27)?*

There will be some awful shocks when Jesus returns and the door to heaven is closed. The way to heaven is narrower than most realise (v 24). The people of Jesus' day who met, listened to and ate with him, but never gave him their trust or allegiance, will be shut out (v 26-27).

Jesus has turned the question around. He focuses us not on "Will the saved be few?" but "Will the saved be you?"

⌄ Apply

❓ *What might you say to people who think...*
- *"I go to church—I'm saved."*
- *"I read my Bible to listen to Jesus every day—I'm fine."*
- *"I'm a good person—I'll be in heaven."*

Weeping

People shut out of God's eternal kingdom will be able to see it (v 28). Outside the kingdom—hell—is a place with nothing good in it. All that will be there is the weeping of regret, the gnashing teeth of self-recrimination. Heaven is real, and hell is real—there is no room for complacency about our eternal futures.

⌄ Apply

As Christians, it's very easy to have a double standard on this—to know we are saved by knowing Jesus, but to complacently allow ourselves to think that others we love who don't know Christ will still be ok.

❓ *Is there anyone who you're seeing in this way?*
❓ *How will remembering that the door is narrow change your prayers for them, and your words to them?*

⌃ Pray

Jesus' words are challenging. But we mustn't miss the amazing truth that people from all over the world will "take their places at the feast in the kingdom of God" (v 29).

Thank God now that, through his Son's death and resurrection, the narrow door is open.

A fox and a hen

Today's passage sets two parallels side by side. Both contain a warning followed by a refusal to respond. But where one ends with only apparent tragedy, the other ends with real tragedy.

Leave? I must keep going

Read Luke 13:31-33

> ❷ *Why do these Pharisees warn Jesus to leave the Jerusalem area (v 31)?*

We're used to the Pharisees opposing Jesus and plotting against him. Here, some of them seem to be concerned for his safety. It's a great reminder that we must not over-generalise about groups and types of people. We should always be ready to see signs of concern for the Lord in unexpected places.

> ❷ *How does Jesus respond to the threat to his life (v 32-33)?*
> ❷ *Why must he reach Jerusalem (v 33)?*

The word "must" is key here. Jesus used the word back in 9:22 when he said he "must suffer many things ... and he must be killed and on the third day be raised to life". Jesus knew he must go to Jerusalem, and suffer and die, because that was what he had come to do. He could have listened to the warning, and turned back and stayed safe—but he resolved to walk on towards his death, his sin-bearing death in our place. His death was no tragedy—his death was his triumph.

▲ Pray

Thank Jesus that he refused to respond to voices telling him to turn back from the cross. Thank him that he resolved to take your place and bear your judgment so he could give you his perfection and eternal life.

Gather: you were not willing

Read Luke 13:34-35

> ❷ *What had Jesus longed to do for the residents of the capital (v 34)?*
> ❷ *Why had he not done this (v 34)?*

And so Jerusalem has chosen to be outside the refuge of God's presence.

> ❷ *What will happen to it (v 35)?*

This is a real tragedy—the greatest tragedy. God's ancient people, instead of welcoming his King and coming under his care and protection, have chosen to reject him and face desolation. Only as and when they realise that Jesus is the blessed one who has come to do God's work (v 35) will they find safety.

▲ Pray

Although the context is tragic, the picture of Jesus as mother hen (v 34) is lovely.

Thank Jesus that his wings cover you—that you walk through life in his care, and that you will come through the desolation of death into his presence. Pray that this would make a difference to how you feel and think about your life today and your future to come.

Food for thought

It's a tinderbox. Not only is it a Sabbath, but Jesus is eating dinner with a high-level Pharisee—two ingredients which often prove explosive!

Read Luke 14:1-6

The dispute, as so often (see Luke 6:6-11; 13:10-17), revolves around what the Sabbath is for. Unlike in the previous episodes, though, here it is only Jesus who speaks. He has reduced his opponents to impotent silence (14:4, 6). So Jesus takes advantage of the lull in conversation to draw two dinner-based word pictures of how kingdom people think and act. The first is about our attitude towards God; the second challenges our attitude towards people.

God's dinner

Read Luke 14:7-11

This is a parable, a word picture—the "host" (v 9) is God.

- ❷ *What prompts Jesus to tell the story?*
- ❷ *Since God is the host, what is he warning people not to do? Why not?*
- ❷ *How should people think of themselves instead (v 10)?*

Deep down, we all want to be respected, or popular, or praised. We would like to think that our own achievements and abilities can bring us success.

The gospel turns all of that on its head—which is why it is so offensive to so many. It shows us that the sum of all we are and do leaves us as a sinner, facing judgment. It tells us that, far from earning the right to sit next to God, we have no right to sit with him at all.

···· TIME OUT ····

Read Ephesians 2:1-7. Having humbled us, the gospel exalts us, showing us Christ, with whom we're seated at God's side. Not because of what we are and do, but because of who he is and what he has done. Yet to be exalted in him, we must first be humble in ourselves (Luke 14:11).

Our dinners

Read Luke 14:12-14

- ❷ *What kinds of people shouldn't be the only ones we ever do anything for (v 12)? Why not?*
- ❷ *What should we do instead (v 13)?*
- ❷ *Why (v 14)?*

We know we have an undeserved seat at God's overflowing table beyond our resurrection (v 14).

- ❷ *How will appreciating this truth lead us to give generously to those who can never repay us?*

⌄ Apply

How do you give to those who can't (or won't) give back? Who are the people, in your church or outside, who tend not to be invited—who people rarely give their attention or welcome to?

- ❷ *When will you invite them to share your table with you?*

Introduce a friend to

explore

If you're enjoying using *Explore*, why not introduce a friend? *Time with God* is our introduction to daily Bible reading and is a great way to get started with a regular time with God. It includes 28 daily readings along with articles, advice and practical tips on how to apply what the passage teaches.

Why not order a copy for someone you would like to encourage?

Coming up next...

Explore 100th Edition

- Luke 14–24
  with Carl Laferton

- Micah *with Frank Price*

- John 3:16
  with Martin Salter

- 2 Kings *with James Hughes*

- Genesis 3:15
  with Sinclair Fergusson

- Philippians 3:10-11
  with Tim Chester

Good Book Guides
Faithful, focused, flexible

3 reasons to try...

1 Field-tested studies that are adaptable for your group: *Optional extras* and *Explore more* sections that give you everything you need to run a short, or longer, session.

2 Extensive help for leaders: built-in leader's notes to help you navigate through difficult questions and passages.

3 Faithful, practical and relevant: great questions that work off the page to take you to the heart of God's word and apply it to your lives.

thegoodbook.co.uk/goodbookguides
thegoodbook.com/goodbookguides